Unless
and
Until

A Bahá'í Focus
on the Environment

Arthur Lyon Dahl

© Bahá'í Publishing Trust 1990
27 Rutland Gate
London SW7 1PD

All rights reserved

British Library Cataloguing in Publication Data
Dahl, Arthur Lyon
Unless and Until
1. Environment. Bahá'í viewpoints
I. Title
297.93171

ISBN 1-870989-09-0

Series editor, Gordon J. Kerr

'The well-being of mankind,
its peace and security are unattainable
unless and until its unity
is firmly established.'

(Bahá'u'lláh)

Arthur Dahl, born California, 1942, obtained his degree in Biological Sciences from Stanford University, and his Ph.D. (Biology) from the University of California, Santa Barbara. He has held a number of influential posts in the environmental sciences – Associate Curator of the Department of Botany at the Smithsonian Institution, Washington D.C. (1970–4); Regional Ecological Adviser to the South Pacific Commission, New Caledonia (1974–82); and independent consultant in ecology to international organizations and governments (1982–9). He is currently Deputy Director of the Oceans and Coastal Areas Programme Activity Centre, United Nations Environment Programme, Nairobi, Kenya.

More than 60 of his scientific and environmental papers have been published in professional environmental journals and official reports, and he was one of the contributing authors to *Mark Tobey; Art and Belief*, an appreciation of the American artist. Arthur Dahl is married, with two children.

The contents of this book reflect the author's own opinions, and may not necessarily correspond with the views of the United Nations Environment Programme.

Contents

Introduction

The end of the Cold War and the thawing of relations between East and West has co-incided with the widespread recognition of new threats to humanity. Holes in the ozone layer, global warming, the destruction of the rainforests, the poisoning of our rivers and seas – all these and more now cause alarm of the kind previously associated with times of war and violent upheaval. This new ecological awareness demands new thinking and new powers of description to deal with the growing threat to our planet. We are no longer merely consumers but polluters: our habits of a lifetime, our domestic, commercial and leisure activities must all now be evaluated in terms of their ecological safety. Whether we like it or not we are all collectively guilty of the crime of 'ecocide' – the murder of the environment. Whereas murder is usually deliberate and often premeditated, today our environment is being killed just as much by our thoughtlessness and outmoded ideas or unwillingness to take action, as it is by predatory commercial and political interests. Governments are only now waking up to the scale of our common plight, while others warn that the clock has already begun to strike midnight.

Our response to this new threat has so far been slow and somewhat mixed. Many individuals are reluctant to accept the need for change, while a few appear only too eager to embrace the role of prophets of doom. Most of us are just plain worried, if not scared: we are willing to make sacrifices but are still unsure whom to trust or believe. 'Environmental friendliness' has become the new touchstone for the products of our consumer society, and political parties of all shades now claim to have a 'green' agenda. Sadly, such expressions of concern often reveal themselves to be little more than marketing hyperbole or expedient political posturing.

Changes of a much more fundamental nature are required – changes which are bound to be painful, and bound to be resisted. Failure to address the real issues *now* can only increase the risk to our future and to the continued survival of different species on our planet, and so deepen the downward spiral of environmental destruction which we have already entered.

The vast increase in awareness of 'green' issues over the past few years has, however, shown widespread acknowledgement of two factors central to the current environmental crisis. The first is that we all must take responsibility for our own actions. This demands a new maturity in our values, attitudes and behaviour in our relationships with each other, and especially with other species with whom we share our planet. The second factor is the recognition that our world functions as one single, amazingly complex yet interdependent system. The forces of nature do not respect national boundaries, nor do man-made corruptions of nature. Acid rain goes wherever the wind blows, as did the fallout from Chernobyl. Ecological disasters will affect everyone directly or indirectly, no matter who or where they are. There is no hiding place. The major threats to our environment are global in their consequences and so must be their solution, but how are we responding to this challenge?

The practical unification of the world and all its inhabitants is inevitable, but it is a process going on largely against humanity's collective will. Political, religious and social leaders are more often responding to crises, than encouraging unification. A few lone voices urge us to extend our vision and embrace the unity of the human race, but the concept is still anathema to otherwise far-sighted decision makers, and sometimes bewildering to the general public. The sheer diversity of human societies, the variety of customs, beliefs, and languages is seen as an insurmountable barrier to human unity. There is also a tangible fear of unity, much exploited by leaders of public opinion, based on the conviction that 'unity' means the loss of identity. This is, however, to confuse unity with uniformity. The establishment of such monolithic uniformity would be a mistaken enterprise without value or virtue, and could never be enforced on the human species. All past attempts to do so have rightly ended in failure, albeit sometimes with a tragic cost in human suffering. We need cultural diversity to build a just and peaceful world just as we need biological diversity for the health and maintenance of sustainable life on the planet. The dominance of one group over another is a symptom of a sick society.

The recognition of the earth as our common homeland becomes more widely accepted every day, but what does this mean if we do not also accept the oneness of the human race? The unity of the world is not just some academic matter of geography, climatology or oceanography, but is about the globalization of all human affairs. It is a living issue involving the hopes, needs and aspirations of real people. It demands a fundamental change in the way nations relate to each other, and requires that the people of all nations work together to preserve our small planet. It also offers a new vantage point from which we clearly see that something can be done to avert impending disaster.

Arthur Dahl looks from this new vantage point on what world unity means for our relationship with the environment. He brings to the subject a wealth of professional experience in the environmental sciences, and an acute awareness of how disruption of the environment affects each kind of human-society, from the industrialized city to the smallest pacific island. He offers a scientific appraisal of environmental problems which goes much deeper than the often superficial populist analysis, while remaining accessible to the non-professional reader. He frankly acknowledges the magnitude of the ecological crisis, and that there are no quick and easy answers, yet at the heart of his book is a vision of the human race at one with the planet, a vision which he expresses through realistic proposals for the permanent solution of our current environmental crisis.

His proposals are based on the writings of Bahá'u'lláh (1817-92), whose insights into the condition of the human race many believe to be without parallel in modern times. Bahá'u'lláh diagnosed the major cause of humanity's suffering to be disunity, and prescribed specific remedies for the healing of human society and of the planet. His teachings have been promoted by his followers, known as Bahá'ís, for more than a century, and are now rapidly gaining currency. Arthur Dahl has rendered an important service by making available for the first time a concise account of those principles and teachings which Bahá'ís see as most relevant to our current environmental crisis, and by describing how the world-wide Bahá'í community is attempting to put them into practice. This list is far from exhaustive, as Bahá'ís, like people of other faiths, are continually discovering new layers of truth and significance in their own beliefs. What is distinctive about the Bahá'í approach, however, is that their concern for the environment is fundamental to their faith and that their agenda for personal and global transformation is wholly consistent with demands being made by concerned environmental groups everywhere. Bahá'ís, perhaps more than any other group, share a practical vision based on a universal ethic which is helping create a pattern for an ecologically benign society.

As demonstrated in the last three chapters of this book, Bahá'ís are united in this endeavour through their common commitment to a number of important principles, which they perceive to be vital to the future progress of the world. These include the recognition of the unity of humankind, based on the fact that people of all races and nations are of equal worth; the establishment of social justice, ensuring equality of rights, privileges and responsibilities for all peoples; the realization of full equality between men and women, bringing a new spirit of feminine values into decision making, including the protection and use of natural resources; the urgent need for universal education which also awakens the compassionate aspect of human nature and a sense of common responsibility for the human family and the earth; the appreciation and encouragement of the wonderful variety of human cultures and the protection of minorities; the balance of individual initiative and social responsibility; a flexible framework of democratic consultation operating at the grass roots of society which places people at the centre of the political process and puts them in control of their local environment; the harmonization of science and technology with spiritual and moral values; a world federal order representing all nations and peoples, free of the evils of over-centralized power, yet capable of maintaining the peace and guiding the progress of world society; a sustainable global economy, organized for the good of all peoples with primary importance given to agriculture, operating within a fair market system which eliminates the extremes of poverty and wealth, extremes which probably more than any other factor are a direct cause of environmental degradation.

Such aspirations and objectives, far from being some ideal notion or utopian vision are, for Bahá'ís, realistic and attainable goals. The pattern of future society which we are asked to consider is an organic one. As Arthur Dahl demonstrates, such organic systems can be found working successfully throughout nature. Decentralized, exhibiting a high degree of local variance and adaptation, the efficiency of such structures have proved their worth over millions of years of biological evolution.

The positive attitude of Bahá'ís is based largely on their own experience of building tens of thousands of culturally diverse but integrated communities, which collectively are united in one organically structured system embracing the entire planet. Although still embryonic in form, this global community is now rapidly evolving into a dynamic model for a world society. Their confidence is also rooted in a profound understanding of the evolutionary processes at work in human society as a whole. According to the Bahá'í view, the innocence of our collective childhood and the trials and tribulations of our adolescent past are at last coming to an end: we are emerging into maturity. Humanity's struggle and sacrifices in the search for justice and freedom have not been in vain, for we are at last coming to recognize our identity as one people. The human race is at last coming of age.

It is on this view of history that the essential message of this book is based. Bahá'ís would argue that it places today's environmental problems in their proper perspective and allows us to see that they cannot be solved through purely 'environmental' activities, important as these may be. The roots of our environmental crisis go much further. It is a symptom of a deeper malaise which calls into question many of the prevailing assumptions underpinning the scientific rationalism and 'objective' forms of knowledge upon which most politico-economic strategies are based. The limitations of such theories of human nature have now brought us to the brink of disaster – and beyond. Millions continue to endure terrible sufferings, and, for many peoples, plants and animals, it is already too late.

In challenging the materialistic and exploitative philosophies which are driving our planet to ruin we can do two things. Firstly, we need to remedy the widespread ignorance of those values which should sustain our relationship with the world around us. Traditional respect for nature, born of intimate contact with her power and immediate dependence on her bounties has all but disappeared. Our appreciation of the beauty and precious qualities of diverse habitats must be rediscovered and strengthened, to the point where even the spiritual value of wilderness is recognized and protected. We must also value and appreciate the wisdom and experience of those cultures and peoples who have learned to live in harmony with their environment. This is not to propose a return to some romantic ideal of the past which ignores our role as cultivator of nature. Such values are not at odds with a modern view of the world. There is no reason why we cannot manage and utilize the environment efficiently by adhering to principles of equilibrium, conservation and sustainability. What is required, however, is an end to the belief that we can continue recklessly to pursue the fulfilment of our immediate desires without reference to the real cost to the planet or to other humans, deprived of basic needs as a consequence of our greed. Perhaps we *can* have it all, but not in the short term. We need to transcend our present consumer mentality and learn how to practice the principle of moderation in all things, including the material development of civilization. Nature continues to remind us of the importance of this law. The rules are quite simple – excess leads ultimately to the deprivation of all. The quality of life must take precedence over quantity of consumption or mere acquisition of material goods.

Secondly, we must rediscover those eternal values and humanitarian principles which have inspired the rise of great civilizations at key points in history. Knowledge of the facts of our environmental dilemma is not enough, we need to do something about it. Our understanding of human nature must advance beyond the shallow, ephemeral view of ourselves as merely physical creatures. Our intelligence and consciousness of our being and action in the world require us to take a longer-term view of our role in creation. Bahá'ís believe that such a view implies recognition of the importance of 'spiritual principles' in the governance of human affairs. In a widely circulated statement entitled *The Promise of World Peace*, Bahá'ís stress the practical importance of identifying these principles in the search for solutions to social problems such as the devastation of natural environments.

There are spiritual principles, or what some call human values, by which solutions can be found for every social problem. Any well-intentioned group can in a general sense devise practical solutions to its problems, but good intentions and practical knowledge are usually not enough. The essential merit of spiritual principle is that it not only presents a perspective which harmonizes with that which is immanent in human nature, it also induces an attitude, a dynamic, a will, an aspiration, which facilitate the discovery and implementation of practical measures.

Bahá'ís believe that such principles, which represent the essence of all religious truth, are within the reach of all peoples and that together we can tackle the root causes of imbalance and injustice which are destroying the life-sustaining fabric and beauty of our world. It is a hopeful vision and one which is sure to be welcomed by all those who share a concern about the future of our planet. If, as they claim, unity is the key issue we must address, then the model offered by the Bahá'í community is one worthy of serious consideration. Through their consistent example and noble vision Bahá'ís are proving that they have a natural role in helping the world overcome those bonds of prejudice and fear which have kept people of different races, nationalities or religions apart for thousands of years, barriers which are now being shattered everywhere.

1. Origins

The environment is everything around us. It is the earth we walk on, the air we breathe, the light and heat we receive from the sun, the stars and galaxies across the far-flung universe, the warmth of our mother's love, the traditions of our culture passed from generation to generation. It is thus possible to talk about the physical environment, the cultural environment, the economic, emotional or simply human environment. Most commonly, however, the term is used to refer to the natural environment that surrounds us and supplies us with everything we need for life.

In some cultures the separation between an individual and the environment is very clear; in others it is blurred or practically non-existent, in the same way that one's ties and identification with one's parents or ancestors may be stronger or weaker. Some Melanesian cultures believe their ancestors originated from something in nature, a tree or shark, for instance, and for them that tree or animal is an extension, almost a part of themselves. People in western cultures feel much more separate from everything around them.

Each human being is an independent entity, but that independence itself depends on our living in a favourable environment. If we are thirsty, we become more preoccupied with finding something to drink, and as our thirst increases, so does our dependence on that aspect of the environment. We are linked to our environment in so many ways that any concept of independence is highly relative. Only the independently wealthy can feel free of the need to earn a living. This illusion of independence is one of the causes of our environmental problems. The poor farmer knows all about closeness to and dependence on the environment. From this perspective, the weather and other aspects of the environment are either uncontrollable or immutable, feared or taken for granted, perhaps open to manipulation or appeasement through the intervention of various spirits or gods. As our societies have become wealthier and more urban, we have lost that sense of nearness and vulnerability. Only the rare natural disaster has served as a reminder of our ultimate dependence on nature.

Today this illusion of independence and mastery is threatened: the poisoning and disruption of the environment is intruding on our limited consciousness and reminding us of our vulnerability. Scientists issue ever more strident warnings about an environmental crisis. Politicians declare environment days and years. The mass media bring reports of environmental catastrophe in every part of the world.

What, if anything, can we do about the environment? How do we relate it to the problems and practicalities of daily life? Is the environment a peripheral concern, or should an environmental consciousness permeate everything from economics to religion? 'Protecting the environment' seems so broad and so vague a concept that it is difficult to see where to begin.

In the Beginning . . .

Interest in the environment is not alien to the systems of thought and belief which have underlain our civilizations since before recorded history. Human beings have always asked where we came from, what is the purpose in being here, and how we should relate to the world around us. There is a considerable concordance between science and religion on the origins of the world, as evinced by many creation myths and stories. Apart from the measurement of time, which is in any case subject to various interpretations, the order of creation as described in Genesis is not far from that supported by modern concepts of evolution. A biologist explaining our origins to a nursery school class would probably tell the same story.

There is one religion which deals directly with the parallels between scripture and modern science. The Bahá'í writings, particularly those of Bahá'u'lláh, the Prophet-Founder of the Bahá'í Faith (1817-1892), and of his son 'Abdu'l-Bahá (1844-1921), antedate much modern scientific terminology, yet their concept of the origins of the universe corresponds well with many present scientific theories.

2

. . . this world of existence – that is to say, this endless universe – has neither beginning nor end.[1]

That which hath been in existence had existed before, but not in the form thou seest today. The world of existence came into being through the heat generated from the interaction between the active force and that which is its recipient.[2]

Modern physics describes matter as made up of subatomic particles with positive and negative charges, and it is the interactions between these in fusion reactions that generate the energy of the stars, including our own sun.

. . . it may be that one of the parts of the universe, one of the globes, for example, may come into existence, or may be disintegrated, but the other endless globes are still existing; the universe would not be disordered nor destroyed. On the contrary, existence is eternal and perpetual.[3]

Science says that the subatomic particles, which are themselves related to energy according to Einstein's famous equation, $E=mc^2$, combined to form atoms with more and more particles, each with their own chemical characteristics, and these elements are the building blocks of the molecules and chemical compounds that make up all material things as we know them. As our solar system formed, the heavier elements condensed into planets such as the earth, which gradually cooled and developed stable conditions. On earth these conditions had the characteristics necessary for the development of life. The Bahá'í writings say the same thing:

. . . in the beginning matter was one, and that one matter appeared in different aspects in each element. Thus various forms were produced, and these various aspects as they were produced became permanent, and each element was specialized. . . . Then these elements became composed, and organized and combined in infinite forms . . .
. . . from the composition and combination of elements, from their decomposition, from their measure, and from the effect of other beings on them, resulted forms, endless realities, and innumerable beings.[4]

3

. . . this terrestrial globe, having once found existence, grew and developed in the matrix of the universe, and came forth in different forms and conditions, until gradually it attained this present perfection, and became adorned with innumerable beings, and appeared as a finished organization.[5]

For Bahá'ís, there is no need to separate the unknowable essence which we call God from the laws of the natural world. On the contrary, scientific laws are themselves the expression of a Divine reality.

Nature is God's Will and is its expression in and through the contingent world.[6]

This Nature is subjected to an absolute organization, to determined laws, to a complete order and to a finished design, from which it will never depart – to such a degree, indeed, that if you look carefully and with keen sight, from the smallest invisible atom up to such large bodies of the world of existence as the globe of the sun or the other great stars and luminous spheres, whether you regard their arrangement, their composition, their form or their movement, you will find that all are in the highest degree of organization and are under one law from which they will never depart.[7]

The classification of the different levels of organization of the natural world into mineral, vegetable and animal, with the latter distinguished from the former by the capacities for growth and for sense perception, is also common to the scientific and Bahá'í world views. However, unlike the views of some scientists, Bahá'ís see humans standing apart from the animal, being

. . . the highest specialized organism of visible creation, embodying the qualities of the mineral, vegetable and animal plus an ideal endowment absolutely minus and absent in the lower kingdoms – the power of intellectual investigation into the mysteries of outer phenomena. The outcome of this intellectual endowment is science which is especially characteristic of man. The scientific power investigates and apprehends created objects and the laws surrounding them. It is the discoverer of the hidden and mysterious secrets of the material universe and is peculiar to

4

man alone. The most noble and praiseworthy accomplishment of man therefore is scientific knowledge and attainment.[8]

Evolution

The concept of evolution, particularly as applied to human beings, has unfortunately become a source of contention between science and religion, at least for some Christians. Yet evolution in its broadest sense is one of the underlying characteristics of the universe and a general law of the natural world as we know it.

Evolution combines the notions of change and of progression, usually in the direction of increasing complexity, although this is not always applicable to particular cases where cyclical or temporary phenomena of progression and regression may mask a long-term progressive trend.

Whether the universe is evolving and expanding, perhaps from a primeval 'big bang' when matter and energy were thrust in all directions at the speed of light, or exists in some steady state, it seems apparent that matter has undergone the evolution described above, with particles forming ever-heavier elements, and atoms combining in ever-larger and more complex molecules. This chemical evolution produced accumulations of molecules which at some point began to take on the characteristics of life, including growth, and replication or reproduction. Some molecules also developed the capacity to absorb solar energy and convert it into chemical form. To survive, these molecular complexes had to acquire protective membranes, becoming the ancestors of bacteria and cyanobacteria (blue-green algae), whose traces can be found in very ancient rocks. Life itself has seen the evolution of ever-more complex forms, as illustrated both in the extensive fossil record and in the enormous diversity of living things which exist today. The mechanisms of biological evolution have now been well established, both through observations in nature and through the example of breeding programmes for domesticated plants and animals.

The Bahá'í writings accept the scientific evidence for evolution:

. . . the growth and development of all beings is gradual; this is the universal divine organization, and the natural system.[9]

However, they make the distinction between the potential for all types of beings, including human, which is inherent in the substance and laws of the creation and has thus always existed, and the process by which that potential is revealed.

. . . as man in the womb of the mother passes from form to form, from shape to shape, changes and develops, and is still the human species from the beginning of the embryonic period – in the same way man, from the beginning of his existence in the matrix of the world, is also a distinct species – that is, man – and has gradually evolved from one form to another.[10]

All beings, whether large or small, were created perfect and complete from the first, but their perfections appear in them by degrees. The organization of God is one: the evolution of existence is one: the divine system is one.[11]

. . . all these endless beings which inhabit the world, whether man, animal, vegetable, mineral – whatever they may be – are surely, each one of them, composed of elements. There is no doubt that this perfection which is in all beings is caused by the creation of God from the composing elements, by their appropriate mingling and proportionate quantities, the mode of their composition, and the influence of other beings. For all beings are connected together like a chain, and reciprocal help, assistance and interaction belonging to the properties of things are the causes of the existence, development and growth of created beings.[12]

Humankind has, by the development of consciousness and of a rational intellect, begun a new process of evolution at the level of culture and civilization. Instead of genetic mutations transmitted by the copying of the complex molecules of DNA during reproduction, great discoveries are stored in libraries and transmitted through education. As we are only just emerging from the exigencies of the

6

struggle for existence, we are only seeing the first glimmerings of the enormous potential of this new level of evolution.

Even religion has gone through an evolutionary series of progressive revelations, by which the founders of the world's great religions have guided humanity's spiritual evolution towards higher and more refined forms of spiritual experience and awareness. These same religions have laid down the social laws and principles which have permitted the restructuring and development of society towards larger circles of unity with greater integration and interaction.

The scientific evidence shows clearly that the long-term trend of evolution at any level, whether biological or social, is towards greater complexity and higher levels of interaction. This process in itself brings out attributes which we often associate with the aims of religion at a social level. As 'Abdu'l-Bahá wrote:

In surveying the vast range of creation thou shalt perceive that the higher a kingdom of created things is on the arc of ascent, the more conspicuous are the signs and evidences of the truth that co-operation and reciprocity at the level of a higher order are greater than those that exist at the level of a lower order. For example the evident signs of this fundamental reality are more discernible in the vegetable kingdom than in the mineral, and still more manifest in the animal world than in the vegetable. [13]

The complex systems that result from this process share certain basic characteristics. They have high levels of interrelationship and interaction among the component parts, expressed in biological systems by the mutually supportive relationships called 'symbioses', and in social systems by co-operation and reciprocity. They tend to high efficiency in the use of energy, materials or human and organismic capacities, with a maximum reduction in losses or wastage. They may also be characterized by what can be called 'dynamic stability', like a gyroscope that maintains its balance because it is moving. These complex systems are open to movement and change while resisting destabilization or disruption. The human body itself is an excellent example of such a complex system.

7

2. The Biosphere

This planet earth seems immense to us, but as the astronauts brought home to us when they viewed it from space, it is just a sphere in the sky. Relative to the immensity of the universe, it is just a speck of dust orbiting around a smallish star (our sun) in a galaxy of millions of stars which is just one among many galaxies. We do not know how far the universe extends. As our instruments get better, we can see farther and farther and have yet to discover any limit.

Our earth is one of the smaller planets, but its distance from the sun and its gravitational field are such that it has retained some gases around it that make up our atmosphere, and its temperature has allowed some water vapour to condense into liquid water which becomes too cold and solid only at the poles. You might say the earth is like a wet football, a sphere solid at the surface and covered by a thin layer of mud and water. It is this thin layer of soil, water and air capable of supporting life as we know it which we call the 'biosphere', the sphere of life.

Within our solar system, the biosphere has a very special combination of characteristics which make life possible. Our distance from the sun is just sufficient for its warmth to maintain water as a liquid. Venus is too close and too hot; Mars too far and too cold. Liquid water is so important because it is a nearly universal solvent, which means that many chemical compounds can dissolve in it. The earth's crust is endowed with a wide variety of elements and compounds. In the solid state, reactions between them are difficult. It is only when they are dissolved in a solvent like water that many chemical reactions become possible. With the help of the constant influx of solar energy, innumerable reactions took place and life evolved. Initially that life survived and developed in the protective envelope of the water in the oceans. The earth's atmosphere was probably composed largely of ammonia and carbon dioxide, a combination hostile to life as we know it. It was the action of living things which made the earth the habitable place it is today. The action of plants over many eons gradually took up the carbon dioxide, separated it into its component elements, carbon and oxygen, and returned the oxygen to the atmosphere. The carbon was incorporated into the plant bodies as organic matter, and gradually laid down in the great underground deposits of coal and oil that we are so busy discovering and exploiting today. The presence of oxygen in the atmosphere made possible the breakdown of ammonia into nitrogen and water, leading eventually to the atmosphere as we now know it. The combination of the relatively inert nitrogen plus just enough oxygen is precisely what we need for terrestrial life.

Today the delicate balance of the atmosphere is maintained by the combined action of plants and animals. This concept of ecological balance was well described over 70 years ago by 'Abdu'l-Bahá:

> Consider for instance how one group of created things constituteth the vegetable kingdom, and another the animal kingdom. Each of these two maketh use of certain elements in the air on which its own life dependeth, while each increaseth the quantity of such elements as are essential for the life of the other. In other words, the growth and development of the vegetable world is impossible without the existence of the animal kingdom, and the maintenance of animal life is inconceivable without the co-operation of the vegetable kingdom. Of like kind are the relationships that exist among all created things. Hence it was stated that co-operation and reciprocity are essential properties which are inherent in the unified system of the world of existence, and without which the entire creation would be reduced to nothingness.[14]

Essential Life Support Systems

The biosphere is maintained within the narrow limits necessary for life through what are referred to, by analogy with spacecraft, as 'essential life-support systems'. These are the global systems that provide one or another of the factors which we cannot live without.

For instance, there is the water cycle. The water in the seas and on land evaporates, primarily through the influence of solar energy. This is a distillation process in which the water molecules go into the atmosphere as water vapour and any salts or impurities in the water are left behind. The water vapour in the air is redistributed around the surface of the earth until it condenses and falls back to earth in the form of rain or snow. The water cycle provides pure fresh water to all the land areas, and recharges lakes, rivers and ground-water. Without the water cycle, all water would drain back into the sea and become salty, and the land would become a lifeless desert.

The atmospheric equilibrium is another life-support system which has already been referred to above. In addition to the balance of nitrogen and oxygen, the air contains small amounts of other gases, including water vapour and a small amount of carbon dioxide necessary for plant photosynthesis (food making from sunlight). These gases help to retain solar energy and thus keep the atmospheric temperature more stable and comfortable. The rainfall of the water cycle helps to wash dust and other impurities out of the atmosphere, keeping it clean. The oceans also absorb atmospheric gases, including carbon dioxide, and so have a role in the atmospheric balance. As a result the atmosphere has remained quite stable for a long period of time.

The driving force for the life-support systems of the biosphere, and indeed for almost all life, comes from solar energy. The nuclear fusion reactions taking place in the sun bombard the earth with radiations all across the energy spectrum, including heat (infrared), visible light, and ultraviolet. Some of these are blocked or reflected by the atmosphere, including the clouds (which are made of condensed water vapour); the rest reach the earth's surface, where some light is absorbed by plants and converted into chemical energy for all life, and the rest is reflected as light or becomes degraded as heat, which ultimately also leaves the earth and is radiated into space. Energy is thus constantly passing through the biosphere, going out as fast as it comes in. When these two processes are in balance, the

10

temperature of the earth remains stable; if the two are unbalanced, the earth either heats up or cools down. One of the miracles of life is that organisms have learned to store and use that energy on its way through the system. One interesting feature of the energy/atmosphere system is the ozone layer. Ozone is a molecular combination of oxygen produced in the upper atmosphere when ultraviolet light is absorbed by normal oxygen molecules. Ozone also serves as a screen preventing the dangerous ultraviolet radiation from reaching the earth's surface. Ultraviolet light breaks molecules apart. It is thus lethal to all life in large doses, and even in small amounts produces sunburn, skin cancer, genetic mutations and other damage. Fortunately the daily bombardment by ultraviolet rays maintains an ozone screen all across the upper atmosphere, protecting us from all but a tiny fraction of this dangerous radiation.

Other smaller-scale cycles also play a role in the biosphere. Nitrogen, for instance, is an essential component of many biological compounds, but few organisms can take it directly from the atmosphere. A few tiny bacteria and cyanobacteria have the capacity to fix nitrogen in chemical forms such as nitrate. These nitrogen compounds can be absorbed and then cycled through the food web, as one organism supplies food to another, providing nitrogen to all living things. Nitrogen is also fixed chemically in factories to make fertilizers. These can increase agricultural yields above those which the natural system of nitrogen fixation can provide. Eventually this fixed nitrogen is broken down by other microbes and returned to the atmosphere.

There are other mineral cycles too numerous to describe here, but all play their role in the delicate balances of life on earth.

Climate

A major global system which affects conditions for life all around the world is the weather system which determines the different climates. This system too is powered by solar energy. It is the heat of the sun, particularly the energy stored and released by the oceans or radiated during the day by the continents, that warms air, causing it to expand, become lighter and rise. Cool air then sinks somewhere to

11

take its place. These movements create areas of high and low pressure in the atmosphere and drive the winds, leading to very complex patterns of atmospheric circulation. Since the oceans and continents have very different influences on the atmosphere, the irregular position of the continents helps to account for differences in weather and climate at similar latitudes around the world.

Climates have not always been the same in the past. The world has been going through a series of ice ages for the last 1.6 million years, when periods of very cold weather brought permanent ice caps to many temperate countries including Europe and North America. We happen to live in an interglacial period when temperatures are much warmer. However in even earlier times, the earth was warmer still, the oceans were higher, and shallow tropical seas covered many continental areas.

We are not sure what causes these major changes in climate. One possible factor is the movement of the continents. We now know that the continents drift across the surface of the earth, driven by the movement of the different plates making up the earth's crust. These plates float on the earth's hot liquid interior. They are added to on one edge by new material rising from the interior, and slide under another plate at the other edge to be remelted as they plunge into the interior. The result is rather like slow conveyor belts under the oceans and continents.

The movements of the continents can be quite spectacular on a geological time scale. North and South America are moving westward at one to two centimetres per year; that is why they have high mountains where they have wrinkled like a carpet along their western edge. Africa, South America, India and Australia used to form one large continent with Antarctica until it broke apart and the different pieces moved north. India collided with Asia, making the Himalaya Mountains. Africa ran into Europe, raising the Alps. These continental movements have changed the relative positions of land and oceans, and the patterns of water movement in the oceans, and this would necessarily produce different climates.

It is possible that there are several different stable atmospheric circulation patterns and climate states, with the system flipping quickly from one to another depending on the position of the land and ocean driving forces or other factors. Although we are making increasingly sophisticated computer models of atmospheric circulation, we still do not know enough about it to say why it changed in the past, or what it will do in the future.

Life in the Biosphere

The stages in the evolution of life on earth have inevitably been influenced by what has happened in the biosphere. There are signs in the fossil record of enormous natural environmental catastrophes, such as that which brought the age of dinosaurs to an end. We do not know for sure what triggered the rapid extinction of so many species. It could have been a giant meteorite impact which threw so much dust into the atmosphere that it produced a sudden cooling, or perhaps some other major change in climate. The giant reptiles which could not regulate their body temperature would have been doomed, while the newly evolved tiny mammals who had developed the capacity to keep their bodies warm were able to multiply and diversify into many species spread across the earth to make up the present animal populations. Many other species have disappeared and been replaced down through the earth's history, but generally very gradually. Different groups may evolve new species very rapidly to fit into new habitats, while others which have become highly efficient at exploiting a particular situation may change very little. One kind of primitive shellfish, a brachiopod called Lingula, goes back over 400 million years. Some common coral species are 20 million years old, and reefs over 2 million years old have many of the same species as modern coral reefs. This is evidence that despite changes elsewhere, conditions in tropical seas have been stable for very long periods of time.

This lengthy process of evolution has produced the rich cover of species and ecosystems across the continents, in the oceans, and scattered on the islands of the earth. There are over 350,000 species of beetles, for example. A single kind of tree in a tropical rainforest may harbour 120 species of beetles, of which half may live only in that species of tree. Considering all the other kinds of insects, plants, animals, and microbes which might be sharing space and resources in the tree, and the large number of different kinds of trees in the forest, there could be millions of species just in such rainforests, and perhaps as many as 30 million species today all over the world.

Each species has some role to play in the ecosystem of which it is a part. For instance, many tropical orchid and bee species have evolved together, with the orchid having a unique form such that only one bee species can successfully feed at and fertilize the flower. If something kills off the bee, the orchid also disappears forever. Most of the world's species are in the tropics. Many of these species are not yet known to science, and their potential benefits and uses have yet to be discovered. Some may be important as biological controls for serious pests and diseases, others may contain medicinally important compounds, or have valuable traits which could be transferred to crops through genetic engineering. Science is only now beginning to develop the capacity to benefit from this enormous natural storehouse of genetic resources.

The great diversity of species in nature is one of the things which makes it possible for natural ecosystems to be so rich and productive. Even our most evolved types of agriculture are still far from the stability and productivity of the best natural systems. This dynamic stability comes from the high level of interconnectedness and interaction in these ecosystems.

The complexity of natural systems viewed at all the different scales of organization and interaction is almost unbelievable. The molecules which make up genetic material are able to store quantities of information in their chemical structure that make our electronic information technology seem cumbersome and primitive indeed. The chemical engineering which has gone into the simplest cell is only beginning to be understood by science, but it is a marvel of efficiency and miniaturization. We are also beginning to discover the complex systems of chemical communication between organisms. Our sense of smell is very poor, so only the strongest odours mean anything to us. However, most other organisms respond to chemical signals in their environment which may tell them when, where and with whom to reproduce, where to live or what dangerous things to avoid. Plants fight veritable wars with chemicals, preventing competitors' seeds from sprouting

14

near them, or giving plant-eating animals or insects indigestion. When we release man-made chemicals into the environment, we have no way of knowing what havoc we may be wreaking on these complex chemical systems. The microbes make up another whole dimension of our environment that we cannot usually see without special instruments. There are bacteria everywhere, in the air, on our skin and on every other surface. The world could not function without them, because they break down organic matter into its inorganic components so that they can again be available for use by living things. Without the microbes, materials cycles would not be complete, dead material would build up everywhere, and life would eventually come to an end for lack of raw materials. Since microbes are always trying to break down any organic material they encounter, living things must be constantly on the defensive to avoid being broken down too soon. Most infectious diseases are struggles between a living organism and some microbe that wants to break it down prematurely. There are also many microbes with whom living things have evolved beneficial relationships, such as those in animal guts which help with digestion. We are thus constantly trying to maintain a delicate balance with the bacteria and other microbes which surround us and are within us, and every other organism is doing the same. This is only one small part of the complexity of any ecosystem.

The higher organisms that are the plants and animals we see around us are another level of complexity in the biosphere. Each one has its own special characteristics and capacities. There are algae that can grow in hot springs, between the ice crystals in the snow, or underneath quartz crystals in desert rocks. Lichens, made up of a fungus and an alga that have learned to live together, are able to survive and grow on the bare rock wall of a mountain cliff and other hostile environments; the algal cells provide the food, the fungal filaments furnish protection. The giraffe has developed a shape which allows it to graze the leaves high in the treetops, beyond the reach of the many other plant-eating animals on the African plains. Migrating butterflies may go through several generations during their annual migration, yet their offspring manage to return, after thousands of kilometres of travel, to the same trees where their ancestors wintered the year before. What are the innate clues which allow them to navigate with such precision? There is no end to the richness and diversity that characterize the living things on this planet.

Yet none of these organisms lives in isolation. All live closely linked with other types of organisms into the many communities we see around us. A forest is made up of trees, shrubs, herbs, grasses, ferns, mosses, large animals, birds, lizards, snails, earthworms, fungi, microbes and many other things. Most would not be able to live alone; it is through living together that they make up the forest community. Yet a forest is even more than a community of many kinds of plants and animals. It has levels of complexity that go beyond its component organisms to make up what is called an ecosystem. An ecosystem exists and functions in both space and time. It is not only the organisms, but all the processes and cycles that tie them together in a complex web of interrelationships. Just as a living body is not just a collection of cells and organs, but is united by flows of blood and materials, and the transmission of nervous impulses and hormones, so an ecosystem is united by the energy captured by its plants and transmitted along its food chains, by the cycles of water and nutrients within it, by the relations that determine the relative proportions of the different species within it, and by many other things, into a single dynamically-balanced functioning system.

The control of biological systems is regulated by an interesting combination of genetic and environmental controls. A plant may carry genetic instructions which determine how tall it will grow and how its branches should be arranged, but these may be modified by information from the environment. If the plant is crowded by other plants, it may grow taller than normal; if it is growing in a very windy place, it may stay shorter and more stunted. Similarly, in an ecosystem, the species selected to grow in a particular place will be those genetically adapted to the environmental conditions present. These may in turn modify those conditions, permitting other species to establish themselves. The environment can also put pressure on the species to select particular genetic changes. Thus in biological systems, nothing is fixed, because everything depends on, can be modified by, and modifies everything else. This is one factor that encourages and maintains the diversity and dynamic stability of biological systems.

The more ancient and highly evolved an ecosystem becomes, the more interdependent become its component parts, to the point that they become unable to survive outside the system. It is the same for any complex machine. All the parts of an automobile work together and depend on each other, yet there are many degrees of dependence. Removing the top will drastically change the car's appearance, but will have no effect on its performance. Unplug the fuel gauge, and it runs just as well, but becomes more difficult to keep going in the long term. Put a bit of dirt in the fuel line, and the whole thing comes to a halt. An ecosystem is the same. The different species may be more or less critical to the overall system, but it is not always evident which species are the most important, just as it is not always clear what is wrong when a vehicle breaks down.

While scientists have been studying the characteristics of species for several hundred years, it is only in the last few decades that much attention has been paid to ecosystems as functioning units in their own right, and we are far from understanding how they work. They are so large and complex that it takes many specialists researching for many years to begin to unravel their secrets.

Yet this is not the end of the problem. These complex ecosystems are themselves tied into larger systems of interrelationships covering whole oceans or continents, involving large scale movements of materials and migrations of species, and all of these are finally linked to the global systems of the biosphere.

The biosphere is regulated by its own mechanisms, some of which have been explained above. It is in its own way as complex a self-regulating system as an ecosystem or an organism. It maintains the correct temperature within narrow limits, organizes the circulation of energy and materials, and recycles or disposes of its wastes, just like an organism. Some scientists have even proposed that it be considered like an organism, and have given it the name 'Gaia', the name of the earth goddess worshipped by the ancient Greeks. The popularity of the Gaia principle has become an influential component of the wider debate over the environment, and can be seen as expressing a widespread search for a spiritual dimension to our relationship with the planet. In any event, this complex series of nested systems from the molecular through the organismic and ecosystemic to the planetary levels which we call the biosphere is as marvelous and as fragile as that other complex system which we know much more intimately, the human body. As Bahá'u'lláh wrote:

> Regard ye the world as a man's body, which is afflicted with divers ailments, and the recovery of which dependeth upon the harmonizing of all its component elements.[15]

Just as we have developed the science of medicine to understand and maintain the health of the human body, so must we develop an environmental science capable of understanding and maintaining the health of the biosphere.

3. Humankind in the Biosphere

What is our place in the universe? This is one of those eternal questions addressed down through the centuries by religion and philosophy, and more recently by science. It is a question which each generation asks for itself, and the answer which satisfies one generation is seldom adequate for those that follow. In part, this is because our concept of the world of humanity, of our very nature, is constantly changing, like the shifting sands in a desert – blown one way or another by the ideas and beliefs of the moment, giving more weight to one aspect or another of humankind's complex reality.

The most evident aspect of a human being's reality is his or her physical being. The human body is, like all other animals, subject to the laws of nature. It has the same requirements for air, water, food, a certain range of environmental conditions, and the fulfilment of certain basic instinctive or emotional appetites. For the hedonist, meeting these needs is all that matters.

Many people today extend this commonality with the animal to our behaviour. They see animals as naturally aggressive, and assume that the aggression and conflict which characterize our society are intrinsic to human nature. This is to misunderstand the nature of aggression in the animal world. Aggression among animals is almost invariably a mechanism for defense, a necessary part of food-gathering, an instinctive process of maintaining a certain population density, or a method for selecting the strongest for reproduction. The purposeless, collectively suicidal aggression of humankind is almost unknown in the animal world. Aggressiveness was perhaps an inevitable concurrent of the struggle for existence, but today we have the technological potential to be freed from the struggle to meet our basic physical needs. As 'Abdu'l-Bahá said, we should be

> . . . free and emancipated from the captivity of the world of nature; for as long as man is captive to nature he is a ferocious animal, as the struggle for existence is one of the exigencies of the world of nature.[16]

This would imply that human aggression is not innate, but simply a function of external conditions and education, both of which can be modified. We are less animal in nature than we tend to think. Correcting this distorted view of our physical nature is one of the essential prerequisites for the establishment of a secure world, as the Universal House of Justice* explained in its statement of 1985 entitled *The Promise of World Peace*, addressed to the peoples of the world:

> . . . so much have aggression and conflict come to characterize our social, economic and religious systems, that many have succumbed to the view that such behaviour is intrinsic to human nature and therefore ineradicable.
>
> With the entrenchment of this view, a paralyzing contradiction has developed in human affairs. On the one hand, people of all nations proclaim not only their readiness but their longing for peace and harmony, for an end to the harrowing apprehensions tormenting their daily lives. On the other, uncritical assent is given to the proposition that human beings are incorrigibly selfish and aggressive and thus incapable of erecting a social system at once progressive and peaceful, dynamic and harmonious, a system giving free play to individual creativity and initiative but based on co-operation and reciprocity.
>
> . . . this fundamental contradiction . . . demands a reassessment of the assumptions upon which the commonly held view of mankind's historical predicament is based. Dispassionately examined, the evidence reveals that such conduct, far from expressing man's true self, represents a distortion of the human spirit.[17]

We have another dimension to our reality, our rational or intellectual capacity, which distinguishes humans from

---

* The internationally elected council which guides the progress of the world-wide Bahá'í community.

animals. The capacity to accumulate collective experience from past generations through education, and to make projections into the future and into other dimensions of abstract consciousness provides us with a whole new mechanism for our evolution. Where the animal is bound by inherited instinctive behaviour and what it can learn in its own lifetime, humans have a much freer choice of the behaviour patterns considered acceptable in the social structure and passed on to the young through education. Aggressiveness is not a fundamental part of human nature, but one of several possible alternative outlets for the anxiety accumulated from the inability to cope with certain situations.

The intellectual reality of humankind, and the science which is its product, make possible what is commonly called civilization, with all that this word implies for material, social and cultural progress. The basic social and intellectual purpose of humanity is the advancement of civilization. We have learned to understand and master the laws of nature and to use them for our own purposes. This has gradually permitted us to free ourselves from the struggle for existence by increasing our productivity so that more time can be available for other things. It has also provided the mechanisms for increasing the scale and intensity of our social integration.

The record of history makes it clear that the biological and intellectual aspects are not sufficient to explain the full reality of human beings. There is a third reality, a spiritual reality, that allows us to rise above the material world of nature. Human beings have never been content with meeting just their physical requirements, or even their intellectual needs. There is a fundamental human desire to turn to something outside ourselves, to transcend our limited human reality and to reach toward a perfection, an absolute reality, an unknowable essence, an ultimate creator or prime-mover. There are signs of this spiritual need in all human cultures, and the history of religion is as old as humanity itself. In fact our first histories are religious.

In the early stages of humanity's social evolution, spiritual questions tended to be subordinated to questions of physical survival. As communities grew in size and complexity, stronger spiritual foundations were needed to provide the common values or moral underpinnings without which stable social relations are not possible. Basic concepts of the existence of right and wrong, of reward and punishment, of the rule of law, of doing to others as you would have them do to you, made social organization possible. More radical were such concepts as loving one's neighbour, turning the other cheek, or submitting personal desires to the will of God or the greater good of society.

Along with this social dimension of religion, which has guided the advancement of civilization, is an individual dimension aimed at the mastery or the emptying of the self, the acquisition of certain qualities, the living of a 'saintly' life, the achievement of 'salvation', the refinement of character, often oriented towards restraint and the development of qualities which would ensure happiness in an afterlife. The universality of these concepts across epochs and cultures shows how fundamental is this spiritual reality of human beings, regardless of the specific form or expression it has taken. In summary, it appears that each individual is launched at birth on what might best be described as a process of spiritual evolution involving the acquisition of qualities which reflect an ultimate 'divine' reality which it is our responsibility to know and to love. In many cultures, the high spiritual precepts set by religion or society were considered to be beyond the reach of most people. There was often a priestly or monastic class which aimed to achieve higher standards, while less was expected of the common people.

Social Evolution

The family was the original biological unit of human society, because the human offspring requires an extended period of adult care and training before it can become autonomous. The development of language and culture permitted the grouping of families into tribes, allowing better defense and more extensive and co-operative food gathering. With the gradual rise of civilization and the evolution of concepts of law and government, more comprehensive feudal systems and cities developed. Certain groups amassed sufficient numbers and power to dominate surrounding groups and to establish empires. The integration of human activities, the development of institutional organisation, and the subordination of the individual to the collective good on a larger geographic scale has led to the modern nation state, whose size was originally determined by the available technologies for transportation and communication.

Each step in this process of increasing human integration has been preceded or accompanied by advancements in the social principles underlying community organization, in the technologies for producing and distributing resources, and in the structures for wielding power and authority. The transitional periods were often times of chaos and upheaval, as old systems and structures collapsed and gave way to the new. Today we are passing through such a period of dislocation and transformation as pressures increase for recognition of the whole world as a single unitary system.

The same type of process occurs in nature. Imagine an archipelago of scattered islands, which gradually becomes populated with different communities of plants and animals by the chance arrival of various species, and by their evolution to adapt to the unique conditions on each particular island. Then suppose that through a major climatic shift or geological upheaval the land rises or the sea-level drops, and the islands find themselves joined together in a single land mass. Without a physical barrier to separate them, the island species would begin to invade the adjacent islands and to compete with already established species. There would inevitably be a period of chaos and confusion. A bird species which originally had all the worms to itself might suddenly find some other bird eating its worms. Several different outcomes are possible. One stronger or better adapted species might replace the other, with the loser becoming extinct. Or the competing species might evolve some compromise; perhaps one would learn to feed in the morning and the other in the evening, or one might selectively eat red worms while the other comes to prefer brown ones. Eventually a new balanced system is established encompassing all the species in the whole larger area.

The same process occurs in human society. The recent discoveries of science and technology have eliminated the physical barriers separating human communities around the world. Modern means of transport and communication have permitted a mixing of peoples and cultures on a scale never before experienced, that of the whole planet. The old human systems, cultures and social structures which evolved in a very different human environment of isolated social units are confronted with the challenge to adapt or disappear. Just as in nature certain rapidly-colonizing weedy species can profit from any disturbance to establish themselves and grow rapidly, before being replaced by more persistent forms, so too have we seen the spread of certain rapidly-colonizing cultures such as communism or American consumerism which have spread rapidly, profiting from the disturbance of the moment. The chaos of this transitional period will continue until new structures are evolved and a new balance struck involving the whole world as a single system.

This whole process of the evolution of civilization has proceeded primarily through humankind's use of intellectual capacity. As far as we can tell, biological evolution of the human form over this period has been minimal. Modern medical science has even short-circuited much of the process of natural biological selection for humans. Most people are prized for their social and intellectual traits, and physical prowess is no longer given much importance.

The Population 'Problem'

One of the characteristics of this difficult transitional period is the extremely rapid growth in the world's population. From 1.5 billion at the turn of the century to 3 billion at the end of World War II, passing 5 billion in 1987 and adding further billions at ever shorter intervals, we are expected under the most optimistic projections to double our population yet again before achieving stability, according to United Nations calculations, in about the middle of the twenty-first century. This explosive population growth has been associated with widespread destruction of resources, increasing poverty, and mushrooming megacities, especially in the developing countries.

We do not know how many people can live comfortably on our planet. Some specialists believe we have already overshot the world's ability to sustain such a population indefinitely. Calculating the earth's carrying capacity depends on the projected level of technology and associated productivity. With present technologies we are already very close to the limits of many resources. Anticipating what future discoveries might make possible is still in the realm of science fiction. However, much of the problem today is less in the total numbers than in the rate of increase of the population, which has outstripped society's capacity to expand food supplies or to provide education and employment so quickly for so many. There are obviously local and regional problems of excessive populations, but this does not yet seem to be the situation globally.

The population problem itself is only a symptom of the imbalances in present-day society. In the past, high birth rates were balanced by high death rates everywhere. Modern science has brought medical discoveries that have lowered the death rate, and with an increased standard of living and better social security, birth rates have also fallen so that many developed countries today have little or no population growth. The rich countries have made great efforts to spread modern medicine around the world, producing a considerable reduction in death rates, but they have not been willing to share enough of their wealth or to correct imbalances in the world trading system so as to raise the standard of living in the poorest countries. The developing world has thus been maintained for 40 years in an unstable intermediate state with lowered death rates but high birth rates, and the population explosion is an inevitable result. Only a global approach to solving the imbalances between extreme wealth and extreme poverty in the world will bring any lasting solution to the population problem which threatens our environment.

4. The Environmental Crisis

The environmental crisis began at the local level. The great London fog of 1952 killed thousands of people. The mercury pollution at Minimata, Japan, affected the local fishing families. The great oil spills of twenty years ago affected tens of kilometres of coastline. Rivers died, like the Thames, or caught fire, like the Cuyaga. Legislation, great expenditure and years of effort have solved some of these problems. London air is cleaner, salmon again swim in the Thames, and regulations and control technologies have helped limit the damage caused by tanker accidents and oil well blow-outs. Those problems, however serious, were still manageable with existing human institutions.

However, all over the world, we are increasing both the rate and the scale of our impacts on the environment. In wealthy countries, new technologies make it possible for the small proportion of the world's population living there to draw on resources from around the world, maintaining a standard of living and comfort undreamed of in past ages. The result is both the rapid consumption of much of the world's resource base, both renewable and non-renewable, and the release into the environment of many wastes, including man-made and toxic substances, that are accumulating in and polluting the global environment. Unfortunately, this rich man's environmental impact is complemented by that of the poor. In the less developed countries, the masses are trying desperately to eke out a living from a limited stock of resources which is rapidly being eroded by the expanding population. When the first priority is to avoid starving to death today, it is hard to worry about tomorrow.

This twofold pressure results in increasing damage to the natural resources and environment, damage that is now reaching the scale of the biosphere. Gone are the days when we could think that the air or the oceans were limitless. The basic life-support systems upon which all living things depend are showing serious signs of stress at a planetary scale.

Despite the rapid development of ultra-complex computer models, we still do not understand the world system well enough to make precise links between cause and effect, so it is not easy to prescribe specific remedies. Scientists are predicting changes that they expect to occur, and in many cases these changes have begun, but we cannot say how fast or how far they will go. Even more worrying, there are often long time lags between cause and effect, so that we may be seeing the results of damage begun decades ago, and the damage we are doing now may not be apparent until some future time when it will be too late to take corrective action. There may also be interactions between different kinds of disturbance or pollution which could either cancel some effects out, or make them even worse, interactions which are very poorly understood.

Atmospheric Problems

Wherever we look today, we find evidence of our threats to our own future. Air pollution has become all to evident in our cities, but the real threats on a global scale are not so evident to the eyes, nose or throat.

The air we breathe has remained reasonably constant in composition since life generated present world conditions. However, the carbon removed from the atmosphere and deposited in the earth's fossil deposits by life in ancient times is now being used to fuel our industrial and technological civilization. Our high consumption of fossil fuels such as oil, coal and natural gas is burning up that carbon and returning it to the atmosphere as carbon dioxide. The amount of this gas in the atmosphere has increased significantly in the last 150 years, from about 2.7 per cent of air in the early 1800s to 3.4 per cent in 1983, and this increase is expected to continue. More carbon which has been locked up in the dense vegetation of the world's tropical forests and other forested areas is also being returned to the air as these forests are cut and burned over very large areas.

Carbon dioxide has a particular effect on the energy balance of the planet. While the light of the sun easily passes through the atmosphere to the earth's surface, the heat that is radiated back out in longer wavelengths is partially blocked by the carbon dioxide and similar gases and held in the atmosphere. This is often called the 'greenhouse effect' because it works like a greenhouse or window that effectively heats an interior by trapping the sun's light. The result of this gradual increase in 'greenhouse gases' is a slow rise in the average temperature of the biosphere, which could amount to between 1.5 and 4.5 °C, by the year 2030. Scientists have predicted this gradual warming of the earth for some time, and the evidence from mean temperature measurements and from signs such as the extent of the winter ice pack near the poles is showing that this increase is indeed taking place.

What are the expected effects of a warming of the earth? Does it simply mean that summer will be longer and winter more comfortable? Unfortunately, the world atmospheric patterns are too complex to be able to say what will happen in any particular place. What is clear is that we can expect changes in climate and weather patterns. Zones of rainfall may shift up to several hundred kilometres towards the poles. Some areas may get more rain, others less. The increasing droughts in the Sahel region and in Ethiopia in Africa are the kinds of changes which might be expected. Such climate changes could have enormous social and economic effects on agriculture and other human activities. There may also be an increase in the frequency and severity of tropical cyclones and other climatological natural disasters.

Planetary warming will also have another serious effect, that of causing sea-level to rise around the world. How fast and how far is not clear. The most widely accepted estimates, assuming a global warming of 1.5 °C, put the rise in mean sea level at between 20 and 140 centimetres by the year 2030, which is within the lifetime of most of those alive today. Some predictions give a sea level rise as high as 4 to 5 metres by the end of the twenty-first century. There has in fact already been a measurable increase in sea level over the last 40 years. Part of the reason for the wide range in predictions is due to uncertainty about the possible melting

28

of polar ice caps and glaciers; we have no previous experience to use as a guide. However, much of the immediate rise will result from the physical expansion of sea water. As water increases in temperature above 4 °C, its volume expands slightly. There is so much water in the oceans that even a 1° rise in temperature will produce a significant rise in sea-level. There is nothing we can do about this effect of the laws of physics except plan for the consequences. And those consequences could be severe. Imagine how even a one metre rise in sea level would affect coastal areas you know. There will be damage to port facilities, flooding in low-lying areas, and increased coastal erosion. The effects will be particularly noticeable during storms, when storm tides and surges may exceed the planned height of coastal defences and engineering works. Major cities like London and Venice will be at risk. Low-lying countries such as the Netherlands, Bangladesh and island states like Kiribati, Tuvalu, the Marshall Islands and the Maldives may lose much of their land area. Low coral islands may become uninhabitable; the fresh-water lens under the middle of the island that supplies wells and makes agriculture possible will be destroyed quickly by any sea-level rise. Their populations will be forced to become environmental refugees.

If global warming continues to the point that it causes the melting of polar ice caps, the rise of sea-level, probably over several hundred years, would be spectacular. The melting of all the ice on earth would raise the sea-level by about 66 metres. Such an event is unlikely, which is fortunate, as it would have disastrous consequences for the flora, fauna and human settlements of the planet.

Another atmospheric environmental problem is equally worrying. We are presently protected from damaging ultraviolet radiation by the ozone layer in the upper atmosphere. Among the many chemicals invented by modern industry are the chlorofluorocarbons (CFCs), relatively inert molecules that are widely used in refrigeration equipment, foam plastics manufacture, and as a propellant in aerosol spray cans. These chemicals have an unusual side-effect; they can cause the destruction of ozone. The large quantities that are now manufactured are eventually released into the atmosphere, where because of their resistance they eventually rise into the ozone layer. Under certain conditions, the CFC molecules finally break down, releasing free chlorine. Each time a chlorine molecule encounters an ozone molecule, it breaks it down, without itself being affected. Small traces of CFCs can thus destroy a lot of ozone. Scientists have warned for at least 15 years of the possible dangers to the ozone layer, but the commercial importance of the chemical industry has persuaded governments to wait for proof. Now holes have been reported forming in the ozone layer over the poles, and they appear to be getting larger, despite some annual variation. The United States banned CFCs in aerosol cans some years ago, and governments have finally agreed to a treaty limiting the increased production of CFCs and calling for an eventual reduction in use as less harmful substitutes are found, but given the time lags in the system, no one knows if this is too little or too late. If the ozone layer thins over populated areas, we can expect damage to vegetation and a rise in skin cancers, among other effects.

A further problem of atmospheric pollution is the complex of problems often referred to as acid rain. Many pollutants are produced by the combustion of fuels, including the oxides of nitrogen and sulphur. The latter are particularly evident in areas burning high-sulphur coal; the former are common in automobile exhausts, among other sources. When these oxides mix with water in the atmosphere, they produce nitric acid and sulphuric acid, with many nefarious effects on the environment. In cities, these acids eat away at the stonework of buildings and monuments, destroying the architectural heritage of centuries. They can render the water of streams and lakes unfit for life. In forests, they may directly damage the tree leaves or needles, or they may accumulate in the soil, changing it chemically, making it less fertile and damaging root systems. The weakened trees are more vulnerable to the effects of diseases, insects or drought, and they die off. In central Europe, up to 70 per cent of the trees are affected, and some forests have been nearly denuded. The future of many European forests is in serious danger, but so much is invested in our industrial and transport systems and energy consumption that it is difficult to see what can be done about it. Since much of this pollution crosses international frontiers, international co-operation is required to control it, but it is not easy to convince one country to incur enormous expenses so that another country may benefit.

Water Pollution

The air is not the only part of the biosphere to suffer from the effects of our industrial civilization at a global scale. The waters and seas are equally affected.

Water is essential for life, and it is constantly cycling through the biosphere, passing from the solid to liquid to gaseous phases. It is solid at the poles and in the ice and snow of glaciers and mountain tops. It is liquid in the rivers, lakes, ground-water and oceans, and is gaseous as water vapour in the atmosphere. Some of our influence is directly on the water cycle. When we cut a forest, we reduce the amount of water vapour returned locally to the atmosphere, and this can change the climate over a considerable area. Irrigated agriculture can have the reverse effect.

The amount of water available in an area is limited by the amount of rainfall, unless water is transported from elsewhere by rivers or groundwater movement, or if fossil supplies of ancient ground water exist, as under the Sahara. The recurrent droughts in Africa have graphically illustrated what happens when a region runs out of water. Some islands in the Pacific have had to be permanently evacuated because the water ran out.

While it is difficult to increase rainfall, it is possible to recycle water. If water is properly purified, it can be reused again and again on its way back to the sea. Many cities drawing water from the lower reaches of rivers are in fact using water which has already been used by many other people. The combination of sewage treatment, the natural purification processes in the river, and filtering and chemical treatment of the urban water supply have again made it drinkable. However, there are always some losses, such as to evaporation, and many places are today running very short of water, to the point that its lack is preventing further development.

More significant on a global scale is the accumulation and transport of pollution in water. The same properties which make water, the universal solvent, so ideal for life, also

31

make it ideal for taking up pollutants. We often use water to remove our wastes, draining the polluted water directly into rivers, lakes or the sea. Other pollutants are washed out of the atmosphere by rain, as in the case of acid rain. Still other pollutants come from the land and seep into the groundwater. Ultimately all of those which are not purified along the way end up in the oceans.

These processes are nothing new, and natural systems have developed many ways to purify the water. Otherwise the pollution, particularly by organic substances, would be much worse than it is. However, nature has never before encountered so many man-made chemical compounds. These new resistant products may simply bypass the natural purification processes, or even worse, they may poison them. The organochlorine compounds such as various pesticides, the toxic compounds of heavy metals, the many hydrocarbon products ranging from vehicle fuels to plastics, are produced today in enormous quantities and released into the environment. Other pollutants such as organic materials and fertilizers may upset the balance of natural processes, causing the excessive growth of certain organisms.

In the past these problems have been localized, but today vast areas are being affected by imbalances that may well have a human origin. Toxic red tides caused by proliferations of microscopic algae are becoming increasingly common in coastal waters, and are affecting rivers and inland lakes. One unprecedented population explosion of algae along the coasts of Scandinavia released toxins that killed off many kinds of fish and seaweeds and affected fisheries and aquaculture along hundreds of kilometres of coastline. The large numbers of crown-of-thorns starfish which have been eating the corals on Pacific coral reefs for the past 20 years may also have been helped to multiply by human factors. Reefs have been overgrown by masses of seaweeds fed on sewage, and tourist bathing beaches are becoming smothered in seaweeds fertilized by agricultural runoff and the tourists' own wastes. Pollution may also lower the immunity of certain animals and render them more vulnerable to epidemic diseases.

Man-made wastes have reached every part of the planet. A team of scientists looking for fish as yet unpolluted by modern industry lowered nets to the bottom of the Atlantic Ocean where water from the Arctic settled many decades ago. In the first haul, they brought up not only some fish, but a ketchup bottle, a tin can, and half a green banana. A second haul some distance away delivered a lump of coal, a wad of oily cheesecloth, and a pair of men's shorts. So much for the unpolluted corners of the globe!

Effects on the Land

The land is also increasingly showing the scars of our negligence. Modern technology has given us the capacity to move mountains and even displace rivers, and we do it all the time, but not always with due consideration for the consequences to the environment. Larger and larger areas of land which were once covered by productive biological communities have been essentially sterilized by human developments. Many cities are situated on prime agricultural land because they started as markets where agricultural products were exchanged. As they have grown, they have paved over productive farmlands with their buildings, cement and asphalt.

The prime productive resource of the land is its soil. A good soil takes hundreds of years to form through the weathering of the underlying rock and the biological action of the vegetation growing on it. The richest soils usually developed under forest. Tree roots can draw up nutrients from deep in the ground, and high forest productivity builds up organic matter to form rich humus in the soil which retains water and keeps nutrients available. When land is cleared for agriculture, those soil-building processes are slowed down or even reversed. Unless special care is taken, the soil will lose humus and start to deteriorate. In modern intensive agriculture, chemical fertilizers are used to compensate for nutrient loss, but there is seldom adequate compensation for the loss of organic matter. Agricultural practices which bare the soil through ploughing or other tillage can also leave it vulnerable to erosion by wind or water. In many areas of the world, soil loss is measured in millimetres or even centimetres per year. The added stress of chemical pollution such as from acid rain only aggravates these problems. The combined result is a steady decline in the earth's capacity to produce. We are living on and consuming the capital stock of soil built up over thousands of years by the natural systems which we have replaced in the name of development.

Look at the present state of the lands which were the granaries and orchards of ancient civilizations, such as those around the Mediterranean, as an example of what can happen. The bare, stony hillsides which have replaced the forests and fields of ancient times suggest that the real downfall of Greece, Rome and Carthage lay in the destruction of their soil resource base through unsustainable development.

In some places traditional agricultural techniques have evolved which respect the land and can preserve its productive potential indefinitely, but too often today these stable systems are being out-competed and replaced by modern agriculture in which maximizing immediate output and short-term profitability are the only criteria for success.

Western civilization may be sowing the seeds of its own downfall through agricultural short-sightedness, that is, if one of our other problems doesn't catch up with us first.

Toxic Materials

Among the great scientific advances of recent decades has been the development of chemistry to the point where we can design substances at will. An estimated 10,000 new man-made chemical substances are invented every year. Many of these have some useful property that leads to their being manufactured in quantity. However, most of these chemicals have never existed in nature, so nature has never evolved rapid biological means of breaking them down and recycling them as it does with the products of natural processes. If they are not broken down by decomposing organisms, they simply accumulate in the environment, subject only to gradual deterioration by physical processes.

The trouble is that many of these chemicals are very dangerous, often in ways which we do not anticipate because we never get around to testing them thoroughly. They may be toxic to living things, often intentionally so if they were invented for use as a pesticide, preservative, anti-fouling compound or medicine. They can also cause cancers, genetic mutations or birth defects, sometimes even when present in very small quantities.

Some effects of chemicals are surprisingly complex. DDT is a classic example. This pioneer insecticide was widely used until it was discovered that it accumulated up food chains, where it interfered with hormonal regulation in certain birds, causing a thinning of eggshells and eventually reproductive failure. The brown pelican in the United States, for instance, stopped producing young over part of its range until a ban on the use of DDT in agriculture gave it a chance to recover. The DDT was draining off the fields and into the rivers and the adjacent coastal waters, where it accumulated in fish, the pelican's food. Similar problems have affected birds of prey such as the peregrine falcon. The inventors of DDT certainly could not have imagined that it would affect eggshell thickness in birds. What other surprises are lying in wait in the thousands of other chemicals being released into the environment?

Dioxin, one of the most toxic chemicals known, is produced as a by-product of certain chemical reactions, particularly when a group of chemicals known as polychlorinated biphenyls (PCBs) are burned at high temperatures. One famous incident occurred in the little Italian town of Seveso, when a fire in a chemical factory produced dioxin which spread over the surrounding countryside, forcing the evacuation of many people. PCBs were widely used in plastics manufacture and to insulate electrical transformers. However, the danger of dioxin production when the plastics were incinerated, and a number of serious cases of contamination when transformers overheated and burned, have caused most countries to ban their use.

Many industrial materials and products use heavy metals such as lead, mercury, cadmium, chromium and copper which are dangerously toxic to humans and other life, at least in certain forms. These also are deliberately released or escape into the environment where they can build up to dangerous levels. The lead added to motor vehicle fuels as an anti-knock compound is emitted with the exhaust, and can accumulate in cities to the point where children who breathe the polluted air suffer from lead poisoning serious enough to affect their performance in school.

The quantities of toxic wastes produced by many industries have reached the point that their safe disposal has become a serious and very expensive problem. Some unscrupulous companies have tried to pay poor developing countries to take the wastes, but poor countries with limited scientific capacity are even less well equipped than developed countries to dispose of such wastes safely; they would simply risk the health and safety of their populations. Many old factory sites and chemical waste dumps were filled with dangerous chemicals at a time when no one worried about the environment. Today their poisons are seeping into ground water supplies or rising to the surface, putting people at risk. It will cost billions of dollars to clean up and safely dispose of this part of our industrial heritage.

Similar problems arise with the development of nuclear science. Radioactive materials are by their very nature dangerous. As they decay they give off particles and radiation that are the equivalent, at an atomic scale, of shooting a bullet into a body; some kind of damage is certain. Different radioisotopes have variable degrees of danger. Some decay quickly into harmless compounds, and once they stop emitting radiation are perfectly safe. Others like plutonium are so powerful and toxic that they should be kept separate from all living things for at least 20,000 years. We have never known a civilization to last 20,000 years.

The disposal of nuclear waste material poses extremely difficult problems which even the wealthiest and most scientifically advanced countries have yet to solve. Engineers optimistically predict that a solution will be found in perhaps two decades. We are thus going ahead with nuclear programmes producing massive quantities of high-level radioactive wastes in the blind faith that science will some day find an answer to the waste disposal problem. Nuclear scientists also assure us that nuclear energy is perfectly safe. After all, the Chernobyl disaster was caused by human error, not a technical failure. But then, has any nuclear reactor not been built and run by humans?

As if these unintentional or short-sighted releases of toxic materials into the environment were not enough, man has also used massive amounts of such chemicals as weapons in warfare. From the poison gases of World War I to the herbicides such as agent orange sprayed over much of Vietnam and the highly sophisticated binary chemical weapons and nerve gases of today, many 'civilized' nations have manufactured large quantities of dangerous materials with the intent of damaging or destroying the environment and human populations of some enemy. We can no longer afford to produce things without asking where they will go and what they will do all during their existence, not only for the first use for which they were made, but long afterwards. We must learn to close the circle the way nature does, and no longer assume that the environment can absorb these things indefinitely. A half-mastered technology is about as safe as a half-cocked gun. The gun is pointing at us.

Non-renewable Resources

The problems of the mastery of modern technology and its by-products are not the only ones facing our industrial society. The West has built a great industrial and technological infrastructure on resources which are inherently limited and are rapidly running out as our consumption of them increases. The heavy industry of the pre-war and early post-war period was built on cheap energy available in fossil fuels; coal, oil and natural gas. The energy in these fuels is basically solar energy captured eons ago by plants whose organic remains became trapped in accumulating sediments. The quantities are inherently limited and non-renewable; sooner or later we shall run out of them, or more correctly it will become so expensive to extract the remaining remote or low-grade residues that it will no longer be worth it.

One recent estimate put the remaining economical petroleum reserves at projected rates of consumption at 60 years' supply. Is that a solid foundation for the enormous investment in power plants, petrochemical industries, transportation networks and other petroleum-based technologies? The difficulties faced by heavy industries, such as steel-making, to adapt to the new economic climate after the sudden jump in energy prices in 1973 illustrate the problem of the inertia in western industrial infrastructure when faced by declining resources and rising costs. Enormous investments have had to be written off. A work force trained for working careers of 40 years is suddenly unemployed but not easily retrained or moved to areas where there are other opportunities (if there are any). Whole regions have gone into decline.

Not all fossil fuels will run out so quickly. Coal reserves will last hundreds of years. There is potential for extracting fuel from extensive oil-shale deposits. New ways are being found to get more oil out of existing wells. But the prospects are still limited, and the economic and environmental costs of some of these processes rise steeply, not to mention the effects of a further increase in the level of carbon dioxide in the atmosphere.

Many other minerals that are basic raw materials for industry are also limited. For a long time, new sources of supply were always being found as geologists penetrated into ever more remote corners of the world. Today there are not many remote corners left. As the highest grade ore deposits in accessible areas are discovered and mined, it is necessary to go to more difficult and expensive areas, and to exploit lower grade deposits, raising the price of the final product. As the prices of raw materials rise, their use becomes uneconomic, and industry turns to some replacement technology, such as the plastics that today are replacing metal and paper (but for how long?). The result again is change and dislocation in the industrial infrastructure. As non-renewable resources run out the rate of change increases, investment becomes less economic, and human social problems increase because the human lifespan cannot be accelerated to match. Building an industrial economy on the shifting sands of non-renewable resources seems to be an inherently risky proposition, and – given the pollution problems outlined above – an increasingly short-sighted and irresponsible one.

5. The Biological Crisis

The more scientists study life on this planet, the more we come to realize how unbelievably complex and marvellous are the biological systems of the biosphere. Life has had thousands of millions of years to evolve into ever more complex forms. In the beginning new species developed to take advantage of new unoccupied environments or habitats. These in turn provided opportunities for others to come after, perhaps to feed on them, or to take advantage of some condition they created, and so on. Relationships between the species were thus established. Not only did species become piled up physically layer upon layer, as in a rain forest, but they also interacted, and came to depend on each other. They have thus formed intricate webs of life, everything tied in with everything else. A change in any one component sends ripples all through the system. Some of these webs are resilient, able to go through great changes and to suffer shocks, but always bouncing back. Others are so fragile and interdependent that the removal of one species may cause them to collapse.

A classic example of the problem of keeping ecological relations in balance is the story of the small Asian village which had a problem with flies. A pesticide was obtained and sprayed around the village to kill the flies. But some of the flies were quite resistant to the pesticide, and they continued to fly around the village loaded with poison. These flies were eaten by the geckos, little insect-eating tropical lizards that walk upside down on the ceilings in the houses. As the geckos filled up with pesticide, they could no longer hold on so well, and began to slip and fall to the ground, where they were caught and eaten by the village cats. The cats in turn began to be affected by the pesticide and could no longer run fast enough to catch the rats. As a result, the village's attempt to control its flies led to a population explosion of rats.

Unfortunately, as in this example, we have introduced changes and pressures of kinds and at scales that are totally outside the experience of most biological systems. A system which is unbalanced or pushed beyond its limits collapses, and is replaced by a simpler and less productive system. It may contain some of the same organisms, but it will not work with the same efficiency and stability. The human effects on the biosphere are of many kinds, some very subtle, with effects that may only become apparent in decades or centuries, others overwhelmingly evident.

Among the latter are the rapid destruction of natural areas and ecosystems all over the world. For many people today, development means cutting down trees, clearing land, profiting from whatever is immediately available. No matter that the soil fertility may decline, the soil wash away, the native species become extinct, leaving behind an unproductive weedy wasteland from which the poor can try to eke out a living: 'Development' has taken place. The rich, those who have profited from development, can go elsewhere and 'develop' some more.

Admittedly this is an extreme picture, true more of the tropics than of temperate areas, and symptomatic not only of ecological but also of social imbalances. Much development does lead to the establishment of productive resources. Many people do find work and a better standard of living. But sustainability is seldom a criterion when development takes place. The true costs, including the environmental, biological and social costs, and the loss of alternative options and long-term economic potential are not entered into the balance sheet. An immediate return on investment is essential, and the future is heavily discounted. The business values and narrow determination of profit as presently practiced in most developed countries are a direct threat to many environmental resources and ecological systems because their time perspectives are so different. Until very recently development projects have not been expected to demonstrate long-term sustainability; a return over five, ten or twenty years is essential, what happens in a hundred years is not considered important. Yet most relatively sustainable productive systems have evolved on the land over generations and even centuries. The European, American or Asian agricultural systems were not created in 20 years.

The passion for development has led to the raping of the land, to the 'mining' of supposedly renewable natural resources, to the loss of enormous natural areas. In Costa Rica, the country with the best record for the conservation of nature in Central America, most of the lush tropical forest has vanished in the last 40 years, leaving only a small percentage protected in national parks. The story is the same in Africa, the Amazon basin, and South-East Asia. The combined pressures of growing populations on the land and of the insatiable demand of wealthy countries for tropical hardwoods, cheap hamburgers and other products are causing the rapid conversion of forest land to other uses. Unfortunately, tropical forest soils are often relatively poor, and such land when cleared can only be used for a few years before the soil is exhausted and the land abandoned. There is little chance that the forest can regenerate on such land.

Sometimes we do not destroy the native ecosystem outright. We may selectively remove just those species that we consider desirable. This could mean logging just certain high-value species of trees, or hunting only certain edible animals or birds. Removing just some elements of a system can unbalance the whole system. Logging the large wind-resistant kauri trees in Vanuatu left the remaining forest more susceptible to storm damage. In some tropical forests, the local fruit-eating pigeons have been hunted almost to extinction. Since these birds were important in spreading the seeds of certain trees, their disappearance means that the tree seeds are no longer distributed through the forest, and the tree species concerned may become less common, or die out entirely.

Another complication has been added to our impact beyond the simple removal of native species or natural systems. Wherever people go, they take with them many organisms which did not previously occur there. Some are useful organisms which we have domesticated: cats, cattle and coconuts, pigs, potatoes and peanuts. Others are familiar and decorative, like roses, goldfish and house sparrows. Still others, such as the common weeds, rats and

41

cockroaches, hitch a ride and come with us even if they are not wanted. Sometimes we have introduced a new organism thinking it will be useful, only to find out too late that it has become a pest, as rabbits did in Australia. Along with all of these have come various diseases; human diseases such as measles, and plant and animal diseases which we have spread around the world. Sometimes these newly introduced organisms may become so well established in their new home that they invade natural areas where they prey on or compete with native species, crowding them out or eliminating them. Frequently a species is introduced to a new area without the diseases and predators that kept it in balance at home; it may thus multiply to enormous numbers in the new surroundings.

The effects of these introductions on the local ecosystems can be disastrous. The unique native Hawaiian forests are threatened by a passion-fruit vine introduced from Latin America. The vine grows up to the tops of the tallest trees, where it spreads out and smothers the leaves and branches. This makes the trees top-heavy so that they are easily blown over in the next strong wind. Other fast-growing weeds fill any clearing in the forest, smothering the new tree seedlings that try to get started, and thus preventing the native forest from regenerating naturally. On islands where many native species have lost the ability to compete effectively, introduced organisms have driven many unique local species to extinction.

Cutting forests and clearing land for agriculture are nothing new, they have been going on since well before the beginning of recorded history. Those parts of the world that have been the seat of civilizations for thousands of years have few natural areas today which do not bear the mark of the human hand. At low human densities, natural regeneration matched human ability to clear the land. But as both development and population growth have accelerated, natural areas have shrunk steadily. In many places, only tiny fragments of formerly extensive ecosystems remain today. As long as such fragments exist, we can always hope to rebuild and extend them to other areas. However, it is these remaining fragments which are now threatened. When they are gone, many species will vanish with them, and they can never be replaced.

We are thus faced with a world crisis in the conservation of nature. The parks and reserves which have been created protect only a fraction of the world's endangered species and ecosystems. Many of these are too small to be viable ecologically in the long term. Others are under threat as poor settlers steadily encroach on them. In countries where land is becoming scarce, planners and politicians are easily tempted to open up protected areas for development. Most conservation efforts have been rearguard actions to save what little is left of natural areas. Some remnants have been saved, at least temporarily, but even these protected areas are not immune to the large scale environmental changes now taking place. In previous epochs of climate change, natural communities could migrate slowly to stay in areas of suitable temperature and rainfall. Today we have so developed the land that there is no place to move to. Ecosystems are trapped in their present positions, vulnerable to acid rain, pollution accidents, even natural disasters. Like a fire whose scattered embers are going out one after another, it may only be a matter of time before many natural communities and species disappear.

The result will be a catastrophic loss of species and genetic resources such as the world has never known, not even at the end of the age of dinosaurs. The world is at risk of becoming immeasurably poorer biologically within the lifetime of many of those alive today.

This is not the only dimension to the problem. The natural ecosystems which cover the planet have succeeded in perpetuating themselves without any problem until now. However, we have so disturbed most of them with species introductions or removals, environmental pollution and other changes, that they have become gravely destabilized. Many of these influences are too recent for their true effects to become apparent. Something that affects the reproduction of a forest tree, for instance, will only become evident when the old trees die off and are not replaced, which may take hundreds of years. Many of these ecosystems will slowly degrade to simpler less productive systems unless we intervene to restore the balance that we have upset. The survival of nature is thus increasingly coming to depend on us. We have unwittingly taken on an enormous responsibility for the management of nature, but

43

we do not yet even appreciate the magnitude of the task. Fortunately the inertia and time lags in most natural systems give us a little time to prepare ourselves for this new responsibility.

At the same time that we are tearing apart the biological fabric which has clothed the planet, we are coming to realize our own dependence on renewable resources for our own future development. The non-renewable resources of fossil energy and minerals are rapidly running out. Long-term development cannot be based on such materials. The only way we can meet the needs of a steadily increasing human population is through the renewable resources of agriculture, forestry, fisheries, aquaculture and the new biotechnologies. But here too the story is the same. We tend to over-exploit or 'mine' our forests and fisheries to the point where they disappear or collapse. Modern agriculture emphasizes intensive monocultures of genetically uniform crops with high inputs of fertilizer in order to maximize short-term productivity. For a pest, nothing could be better than to find so much delicious food in one place. The pests and diseases multiply accordingly, requiring heavy doses of pesticides to maintain some semblance of balance. Such systems are inherently unstable and probably not sustainable in the long term. Researchers try to keep one step ahead of rapidly evolving and increasingly resistant pests. The soil structure and fertility is often degraded under such intensive use. Excess chemicals wash off the fields and pollute the water. Both the highly mechanized cultivation and harvesting, and the chemical inputs of fertilizers and pesticides, involve high energy subsidies to build and run the machines and to make the chemicals. In some cases more energy may be put into the crop in such subsidies than is taken out in food value. As fossil energy supplies diminish and prices increase, this type of agriculture will become uneconomic. In many developed countries it is already maintained only by heavy government subsidies and increasing farm debt.

Despite its negative environmental effects as currently practiced, agriculture is and always will be the foundation of material civilization. Though traditionally given low social status, the farmer is accorded a high position in the Bahá'í teachings. 'Abdu'l-Bahá asserts that '. . . the peasant

44

class and the agricultural class exceed other classes in the importance of their service'[18] because, 'The fundamental basis of the community is agriculture – tillage of the soil.'[19] He describes agriculture as 'a noble science',[20] and encourages both women and men to engage in 'agricultural sciences'.[21] He states that should an individual 'become proficient in this field, he will become a means of providing for the comfort of untold numbers of people'.[22] Bahá'u'lláh characterizes agriculture as 'conducive to the advancement of mankind and to the reconstruction of the world'.[23]

Food is our basic, irreplaceable energy source. As we exhaust the fossil supplies of energy and chemical feedstocks, solar energy newly captured in part through agriculture will have to replace these ancient reserves. We are still far from knowing how to do this sustainably. The examples and genetic resources of natural ecosystems will be essential if we are to make the necessary advances.

All these things together are leading to a biological crisis of unimaginable proportions, with a great reduction in the richness and productivity of natural systems, and inevitably also in the potential for human use of natural resources.

Little can be done to avoid this crisis. The inertia in both human societies and natural systems is too great. At the very least we must make an enormous effort in our conservation of nature over the next decade or two. This will require not only a great increase in parks and other protected areas where nature still has a chance, but also a much more comprehensive approach to managing the systems of the biosphere. Great advances will be needed in our scientific knowledge of biological systems, far beyond the simple biotechnology of today oriented to single species and single products. We shall need to become masters in the restoration and management of whole ecosystems. The present trends in agricultural research towards agroforestry, organic farming, reduced tillage, biological controls and integrated pest management are some early steps in the right direction.

There are of course ongoing efforts to slow the rate of biological destruction. The World Conservation Union (IUCN) has worked for 40 years in defence of the natural world. Together with the World Wide Fund for Nature (WWF) and United Nations agencies, it launched a World

Conservation Strategy in 1980 which has now been reflected in some 30 national conservation strategies, aiming to protect species and ecosystems, to conserve basic life support systems, and to maintain genetic diversity. Following in the pioneering footsteps of Richard St Barbe Baker and his 'Men of the Trees', tree planting campaigns have spread around the world through national programmes and local groups. International legal conventions control trade in endangered species, protect wetlands, manage migratory species, regulate fisheries, control marine pollution and ocean dumping, and provide regional frameworks for environmental action. But these efforts are far short of what is needed. They may have slowed the rate of destruction, but they have not turned the tide.

One of the most encouraging signs is the increasing public awareness and concern over the loss of species and habitats. More and more individuals are demanding action to safeguard and preserve natural environments from the ravages of 'progress' and 'development'. A growing number of conservation, environment and consumer action groups are emerging at grass roots level. In many countries these groups have made a profound impact right across the political spectrum, forcing environmental issues to the forefront of the political agenda. Such groups have an invaluable part to play, not only in educating their own members and others about the damage being done to our biological world, but also collectively as they learn to articulate their concern and express informed opinions they can, as they unite, create powerful pressure groups at local, national and international levels.

Although such organisations often have separate agendas and reflect many shades of political opinion, one hopes that an underlying commonality of interest will enable them to submerge their differences, and more fully exploit the power of unity. Such a step perhaps depends upon the realization that none can escape the disastrous consequences of our blind meddling with nature. Even this however, Bahá'ís would argue, is not enough. To have any real measure of success we require a more positive motivating force than mere fear of the future.

46

6. Where Are We Going?

Human beings have always wanted to know about the future. Fortune telling is one of the most ancient occupations, although today it tends to be called 'advanced projections' or 'futurology'. It is a field particularly open to charlatans and quacks because one cannot be proven wrong until it is too late. At the same time it is important to have some idea of what the future may hold for us. The world is changing at an ever increasing speed; the only thing that is not accelerating is the length of a human generation. In the past one could be trained for a lifestyle and occupation that would remain reasonably constant. Today anyone in Western society who is not periodically retrained risks becoming quickly outdated and unemployable. We need to anticipate change as much as possible in order to be able to adjust to it.

Predicting the future is not easy, as so many past failures attest. One technique that is frequently used is called 'extrapolation'. You determine a trend from the past to the present, and assume that the future will bring more of the same. This straight line extrapolation unfortunately cannot take into account the unknown or unexpected. An interaction with some other factor, a new discovery, or a war can make a projection meaningless. The next step beyond the simple technique of extrapolation is the computer model. Computer models are usually based on projections, but they can be programmed to take interactions between projections into account. It is also possible to vary the projections and see how sensitive the result is to different possible changes in the future.

One of the first attempts to model our environmental future twenty years ago was the classic study *Limits to Growth* sponsored by the Club of Rome. In this study, world trends in economic development, population growth, resource utilization, pollution and other factors were projected into the future, and the computer was asked to say what would happen to our civilization. The reply was that we would advance to a certain point in the next century, and then civilization would collapse as we met some limit to growth. Adjusting one factor or another advanced or retarded the time of the catastrophe, but did not prevent it.

This model was criticized as being too simplified and not taking into account regional differences. Other models were then developed which softened the conclusion, but did not entirely avoid it. All these models were basically extrapolations of present trends. Clearly the world could not continue on the same course; major changes in direction were essential, and indeed inevitable since the models could not anticipate changes in technology or social and political responses to problems. Unfortunately, while the models could say what changes were necessary, such as reducing the population growth rate or halting pollution, they could not say how to bring about these changes.

Future Trends

In the light of the studies which have been done, what are some of the reasonable assumptions about our future? A major problem is the growing human population. The United Nations has made projections for population growth, assuming a continued reduction in birth rates as rising living standards and family planning programmes have more impact. They expect that the 5 billion people who inhabited the earth in 1987 would become 10 to 14 billion before the population stabilizes sometime in the next century. Most of this growth will be in the poorest developing countries which are least able to absorb a doubling of their population. This population growth will bring with it increasing problems of grinding poverty, famine, resource destruction, uncontrolled urbanization, and social and political instability.

The biological trends are also reasonably clear. There will be a continuing spread of simplified, degraded, weedy communities and secondary regrowth on land which has been used and abandoned. Rich, undisturbed, natural

48

systems will become increasingly rare. Signs of large-scale imbalances such as mass outbreaks or die-offs of organisms will become common, and there may be a collapse in the productivity of some natural systems.

There are persistent signs of similar imbalances in the world economic system. The inability of governments to manage what has become a world economic system on the basis of national mechanisms and policies is leading to increasing economic instability. Low prices for the primary products of the third world leave them deeper in debt, and that debt keeps climbing to new record levels with no possibility of reimbursement in sight. There is even instability among the wealthy countries, for whom domestic priorities win out over international responsibilities, leading to enormous debt and balance of payments problems. Here also there is a risk of collapse, or at least of great stresses and chronic problems.

Then there is the continuing risk of a nuclear holocaust. Such an event would – to say the least – upset all the predictions and extrapolations about the future. Most studies of the consequences of nuclear war suggest that between one and two thirds of the world's population would die directly from the effects of explosion and radiation, or indirectly from the collapse of the world system accompanied by famine and disease which would inevitably follow. The dust and smoke thrown into the atmosphere by even a limited nuclear exchange would turn day into night for weeks or months, with a sharp drop in temperature which some have likened to a 'nuclear winter'. The result would be the failure of most biological productivity and agricultural systems, leaving the world without food. It would take decades to recover from such a calamity, and there would certainly be no more population problem for some time to come. Major parts of the countries involved would be uninhabitable for decades if not generations. Bikini Atoll in the Pacific was used for nuclear weapons tests in the late 1940s and early 1950s, and in spite of strenuous cleanup efforts, it is still considered too dangerous for human residence.

Clearly the world cannot continue the present trends and international anarchy forever. The story is told of a man who jumped off a 100 storey building. As he fell past the

50th floor, he said to himself: 'Ah, life could not be better. The view is superb. There is a gentle breeze. Who could want for more?' We are rather like that man, enjoying the present moment and giving no thought to the future, or to the painful landing which awaits us some day.

No trend goes on long in the natural world before some control mechanism comes into play. An excess in prey leads to a growing number of predators, or some other control such as famine or disease. The same is true in the social world; an overdrawn bank account brings a warning from the bank, if not a closed account. Some control mechanisms are already at work. The generally rising price of energy despite short-term fluctuations due to market manipulations, and the scarcity of certain raw materials, have led to a crisis in heavy industry, with massive unemployment. Famine is reducing populations which have exceeded the capacity of their land to feed them.

Prospects for Change

The present structures of the world have shown themselves unadapted to the search for global solutions which are necessary to solve today's problems. It is not possible to manage a physically united world with the anarchy inherent in the concept of 'sovereign' nations. The institutional structures of today are like cultural dinosaurs. They evolved in a different, more fragmented social environment, but that environment has now changed to a single world system. The structures of the sovereign nation, like the dinosaurs, must either evolve or perish.

Fortunately there are great pressures on governments for change, and the environment is one of them. These problems were first addressed globally by governments at the United Nations Conference on the Human Environment in Stockholm in 1972. That conference led to the founding of the United Nations Environment Programme (UNEP) which has undertaken many actions for the protection of the global environment.

For example, the UNEP Regional Seas Programme has built up regional activities around the world for the protection of the marine and coastal environment. In these regional programmes, countries of widely different political persuasions, including those which are actively hostile

50

or even at war with each other, find a common interest in working together to protect their shared marine environment. The scientific reality of the unity of their resources wins out over even the strongest political forces. The governments have similarly started to work together under UNEP auspices to reduce gas emissions that endanger the ozone layer, and to control international trade in hazardous wastes. This is a small start to an enormous set of problems, but at least a start has been made.

The report of the United Nations-sponsored World Commission on Environment and Development, often called the Brundtland Report after its chairwoman, Gro Harlem Bruntland, the then Prime Minister of Norway, has laid out clearly the challenges to the world community. The report, *Our Common Future*, emphasizes the need to reorient the world economic system towards sustainable development.

The growing scientific evidence that the world is seriously threatened by human impacts on natural systems, such as greenhouse gases causing global warming and chemical attacks on the stratospheric ozone layer, have finally pushed the environment to the top of the political agenda. In local and national elections, at international conferences and gatherings of heads of state, the environment has become a major issue, and calls for action are increasing. States which a few years ago were zealously defending their national sovereignty now talk about the need to give up some sovereignty in the interests of international management of global environmental problems. However, while the need for action is clear, the kinds of actions and the directions they should take are far from agreed.

Future Steps?

If we start from the assumption, argued cogently by Bahá'ís for the last hundred years, that the next step in human social evolution is a world society, we can ask what such a future might offer, in terms both of correcting present environmental problems and of building a new resource base for civilization. The author's own view of how the environment might be rescued and developed is based on Bahá'í principles and scientific evidence. Each application of Bahá'í principles opens up new possibilities for society, as does each new scientific discovery. The future will inevitably be richer and more varied than the one presented here: what this scenario does show, regardless of the details, is that a positive future for the environment is possible.

The recent period of rapid technological development and social change has seriously upset the environmental equilibrium of the planet. It is clear from a scientific assessment of the situation that we shall have to repair as much as possible of the damage which our present society has wrought in the world. Restoring the stability of the life-support systems of the atmosphere will require that we re-establish plant and animal communities over as much of the earth's surface as possible. Often this will just involve removing the causes of a problem and assisting the natural healing processes which are fortunately common in nature.

For the ozone layer, for instance, we shall have to stop manufacturing and emitting chemicals that catalyze ozone destruction. Governments have already adopted a time-table for the elimination of CFCs by the end of the century, and the rush is on in industry to find safer substitute materials. Existing stocks will have to be collected and broken down into harmless products. Once the ban is in force, those chemicals already in the atmosphere will slowly disintegrate. After perhaps a hundred years, if present projections of the persistence of these chemicals are accurate, the ozone layer should return to its former density, since the processes which create ozone have been unaffected.

Many biological communities, particularly in more temperate areas, are also quite resilient. As long as the native organisms are still present, and pollution and other outside influences are removed, natural processes of succession will allow the gradual return to something approaching a natural system. Regeneration should be encouraged in all areas not actively in human use.

For other problems, some direct intervention will be required. Solving the problem of global warming and the resultant climate change and sea-level rise will require major reductions in human emissions of carbon dioxide, methane and other greenhouse gases. This will mean a complete revolution in the basic energy supplies for our civilization, replacing fossil fuels with other energy sources. Governments are already considering a global convention on the atmosphere as a framework for applying appropriate controls. Deforestation will have to be halted, and forests, coral reefs and similar communities which are good carbon sinks will have to be restored wherever possible to absorb carbon dioxide out of the atmosphere.

It will be necessary to collect and neutralize or isolate all those products which represent a continuing danger to human and natural systems, such as toxic wastes, concentrations of pollution, and radioactive materials. This in itself will be an enormous task, given the quantities of such materials which we have manufactured and the carelessness with which we have strewn them across the landscape.

The vast areas where the soil surface has been damaged or despoiled will require restoration, first by recreating natural surface contours, then by re-establishing some succession of biological communities capable of rebuilding surface soil. Such processes are slow, and it may take decades or centuries before some areas recover to something close to their natural productivity.

International action is also being planned to protect the biological diversity of the planet, with mechanisms for sharing the responsibilities and costs of preserving these resources in the global interest. Where we have introduced invasive or aggressive species which have upset natural systems and prevented natural perpetuation or regeneration, we shall need to try to eliminate those species, or barring that, to introduce biological controls that will keep them in balance with the other components of the system. Some ecosystems may require that we continue management measures indefinitely if we want to avoid losing unique species or essential components of the system. This may be particularly true of fragile island ecosystems, or of ecosystems which have been reduced to a fraction of their original size.

Some things may take a very long time to restore. Where ground-water has been contaminated by pollutants, it may take hundreds or even thousands of years for those contaminants to work their way out of the system. Similarly, populations of slow-growing species will not recover quickly even with extra assistance. In many cases, the damage done will prove to be irreparable. Where species have gone extinct, they cannot be re-created. Even if genetic engineering made it possible in theory to manufacture a species, we do not know enough about those which have disappeared to know what to re-create. Pollutants diluted throughout the oceans are also beyond recovery; we can do nothing about any continuing noxious effects they may have.

Reasons for Hope

In spite of the losses and irreparable damage which this age has inflicted and continues to inflict on the biosphere, the longer term future is still very bright. Once we have passed through this present age of transition, it should be possible to re-establish the essential foundations for the biological systems of the planet in, say, one hundred years, assuming a general effort on the part of society. From that foundation, a new world civilization can be built surpassing anything known to date. Such a civilization will have to be planned to be sustainable over a period of perhaps 500,000 years – a time-scale greater than even professional futurologists care to think about.

We can try to envisage some of the characteristics of that civilization. Its essential foundation will be agricultural, using the biological resources of the planet, not merely simplified and exploited as they are today, but integrated into complex ecosystems of which humankind will form an integral part. Our existing agriculture based on unstable monocultures will be replaced by complex, diverse and stable systems able to produce all the food and raw materials and a major part of the energy required by society. There will be a great diversity of such systems adapted to all environmental situations on the planet. Each will not only provide resources for the community it supports, but also will absorb and recycle the wastes of the community in an efficient system much like that of the coral reef. With the development of biotechnologies, agriculture and industry will become completely integrated into the same productive system. Since it will be desirable to utilize

54

to the maximum the incoming solar energy, all available surfaces will be put to productive use. The sterile cement and asphalt of today's urban areas may be replaced by an urban forest of trees and plants which would not only surround us with the beauty of nature but also provide useful materials and services.

In such a society, perfected systems of communications and transportation will render obsolete the need to crowd together in large cities. On the contrary, since energy and materials sources will be diffusely distributed across the countryside, the human population could likewise be more widely spread. Community size will probably be determined by what the local resources can support and by what is the most agreeable size for social interactions. A community of a few thousand, for instance, would be large enough to provide basic social services such as education satisfactorily and economically, while permitting everyone to know everyone else, and thus be integrated fully into the life of the community.

With the potential released by the high integration in such a system, growth would be limited only by our ability to increase the productivity and efficiency of the ecosystem of which we would form a part. If we take the coral reef or the tropical rain forest as examples of what is possible, those limits are far above anything we know today.

At such a crucial point in history, when ecological problems are building towards a crisis of world proportions, one could be tempted to dismiss such visionary exercises as utopian. To believe that we can change our ways, that the human race is capable of developing a sustainable and positive relationship with the earth is a stimulus to action: but having such a vision is not enough. The real challenge of our times is not so much to define where we should be going, as how we are to get there – the end is not more important than the means.

7. A Framework for Ecological Values

Viewed within the narrow context of the environmental sciences, there are few grounds for hope for the future. Despite a belated political awakening, it is not certain whether the powers that be are ready to make the radical changes necessary to respond in time to the environmental crises. The inertia of present day society, the powerful forces at work, the sheer scale of the problems involving the daily actions of billions of people, are all pushing the planet towards environmental destruction. While natural systems are amazingly resilient, they must have breaking points somewhere. It is hard to see what can stop the downward spiral in which we find ourselves, short of those ancient scourges, warfare, famine, drought, and pestilence – the ultimate biological controls on the human race.

Yet when environmental problems are seen within the larger context of human social evolution, the forces which seem to be pushing our society to catastrophe may not in fact be following a straight extrapolation. Rather, they are symptoms of those forces of transition which are breaking down the old structures of a fragmented world of sovereign nations so that they can be replaced by new types of social organization adapted to a united world. Some of the most destructive pressures, such as population growth, are in fact produced by the imbalances of this transitional age.

From this perspective, we should expect rapid change in all aspects of our existence: technological, social, political, and spiritual. This also suggests that the real solution to our environmental problems lies not in a technological fix for this or that source of pollution or a new approach to resource utilization (although these are certainly neces-sary), than in the restructuring of world society itself and of the basic values by which people live. Without structures and values adequate to the global environment as it is evolving today, trying to resolve the major environmental problems of the world is like treating cancer with a bandaid. Once a new system is established, the solution of all the subsidiary problems will still be painful, but will be relatively straightforward.

The twentieth century has witnessed the remarkable extension of social systems claiming to have the solutions to our problems. Proponents of western capitalism on the one hand, and of communism on the other, have claimed that they can fulfil all humanity's needs. Just as weeds establish themselves quickly on disturbed land, so have these social and economic systems spread widely around the world, profiting from the cultural disturbances created in this age of transition. Yet both of these systems are basically materialistic in their orientation and ignore or repress other needs and desires. Both have failed to deliver their promises, leading to disillusionment, apathy and loss of hope for the future.

World Unity

If these systems have failed, what are the characteristics of a workable pattern for future society? Obviously the unity of the human race in a single world system – the central fact of this latest stage in our evolution – must be the guiding principle. No system that preaches division or domination, or that ignores the global requirement for justice and solidarity, can meet the needs of the modern world.

An extension of this central idea of unity is recognition of the value of unity in diversity. There is a fantastic richness to the human experience. There are so many human adaptations to the diversity of the world environment, diversity of climates, resources, and geographic situations. Culture is humankind's response to the environment. The challenge of survival in the deserts of Australia or Africa, in the icy wastes of the far north, on tiny islands lost in the Pacific or in great multitudes on the plains of Asia has brought out so many different qualities, social structures, languages and arts, sciences and technologies. These are our human heritage, the products of many thousands of years of social and cultural evolution.

Too often these differences have been a source of prejudice, of fear and misunderstanding, of war and genocide. Today they must be appreciated for what they are, and what they say about humanity's infinite capacities. They must be preserved and enriched as contributions to a world civilization. No biological system could survive with a single species. It is the richness of different species, each adapted to a specific environment or function, which gives the system its productivity and stability. The same is true for the diversity of human cultures; they are the raw material of a future world civilization.

The future world society must also be characterized by a balance of the physical, intellectual and spiritual dimensions of our nature. Today's society is fragmented. Some people are materialists, devoted to the pursuit of wealth or hedonistic pleasure. Others are scientists, artists, intellectuals, finding their satisfaction in advancing the world of ideas, knowledge and the arts. Still others follow the religious life as priests, clergy or active lay members of the church. Yet since body, mind and spirit are all essential aspects of every human being, to emphasize one at the expense of the others is to risk falling into excesses of indulgence, intolerance and fanaticism. The true fulfilment of human potential requires the harmonization of all aspects of human nature, individual and social.

One essential application of such harmonization will be a renewed accord between science and religion. Science is obviously essential if we are to solve the problems of the physical world. The advancement of material civilization is founded on science and technology. Yet science lacks a value system that could permit it to make moral judgements. Science is morally neutral. It can as easily be used to create a hydrogen bomb as a radiation treatment for cancer. Science without the moral guidance of religion falls into the slough of materialism, and becomes prey to innumerable abuses. The role of religion has always been to provide the moral foundations for society, the common human values on which a community agrees and on which it bases its social organization. Today, however, religion is considered irrelevant by great masses of people, whose perception of the world is dominated by material civilization built on science and technology. On the other hand, religion which ignores science falls into the mire of superstition. If those who hold religious beliefs want to contribute to contemporary society, they must come to a new understanding with modern science.

This balance of faith and reason, the harmonization of spiritual and material needs, is at the very root of the Bahá'í outlook. Whereas science and technology have an indispensable role in the reconstruction of human society, Bahá'ís assert that they must be redirected towards the alleviation of material hardship and the promotion of greater equality and unity, through constructive and non-aggressive means.

Science and technology today offer the means virtually to eliminate poverty throughout the world, and allow the physical aspects of life to be given proper attention. For the masses of the poor, physical survival is an all-consuming preoccupation. The struggle to survive can bring out the worst in our nature, particularly where religion has become so weakened that it no longer serves as a control on our baser instincts. Barriers to the solution of the extremes of wealth and poverty are social and political. Change is required, a rearrangement of priorities, whereby politics are governed by just principle as well as by law. A world society, organized on global principles, could lift people above the desperate effort to eke out an existence, freeing them to seek a better balance in their own lives and that of their communities. For the wealthy too, physical nature has become dominant. The pursuit of material pleasure, of sexual gratification, of social acceptance through material possessions, are the dominant motivating forces for many today. This new value system has been both created and reflected by Hollywood and the mass media, by advertising, conspicuous consumption and planned obsolescence. Again it is the animal nature which predominates. Lip service may be paid to the intellectual and spiritual qualities that distinguish humankind, but most people still act in accord with the belief that real power and worth lie elsewhere.

This preoccupation with material advancement has pushed us to try everything that will make money. It has led us into excesses which are at the root of many environmental problems. Bahá'u'lláh warned a hundred years ago of the dangers of this course.

> The civilization, so often vaunted by the learned exponents of arts and sciences, will, if allowed to overleap the bounds of moderation, bring great evil upon men. . . . If carried to excess, civilization will prove as prolific a source of evil as it had been of goodness when kept within the restraints of moderation. . . . The day is approaching when its flame will devour the cities . . .[24]

The increasing problems of pollution and waste disposal, the technological development of warfare, runaway urbanization, the destruction of resources and destabilization of ecosystems, all are evidence that humankind is suffering the consequences of ignoring this warning.

The natural systems of the biosphere can cope with a certain amount of human interference, but only up to some maximum tolerable level. Thus many types of development may be appropriate in moderation, yet today the limits to development are determined more by what can be sold than by what the environment can tolerate. We shall need to learn to use technologies more selectively, to evaluate them in a longer time perspective, and to make sustainability an essential criterion.

Ecological Values

Any fundamental human change must start with the individual. We each share some responsibility for the state of our community, and of the world, and we are fully responsible for the example we set in our own lives. It is at this individual level of basic values that the relationship between science and faith, between ecological and spiritual values, becomes clear.

The intellectual or rational capacity of humankind distinguishes us from all other forms of life. With it we have developed science and technology to the point where they have short-circuited the natural mechanisms of biological evolution. With modern medicine, the survival of the fittest has been replaced, at least in most Western hospitals, by the survival of the wealthiest. Since wealth is not a genetically-inherited characteristic, this survival has no evolutionary value. In fact, since wealth tends to be

60

associated with lower birthrates, the wealthy on this planet are rapidly being swamped by the masses of the poor.

Today our evolution is potentially under our own conscious control. We must decide how we want to use that control, and to what ends. These are moral questions to which science cannot provide satisfactory answers. It was science, after all, which supported Nazi concepts of racial purity and all the moral abominations that followed, including genocide, and it is science which today underpins the military and industrial structures threatening our collective survival.

The first fundamental step is to arrive at a definition of our purpose. Why are we here? What should we be aiming to achieve with our lives? Answering such questions has been one of the traditional functions of religion.

The Bahá'í view of humanity's purpose is a beautiful balance of the scientific and the spiritual. For Bahá'ís, all human beings have both an individual and a social purpose. Each individual is born into this life with many potential qualities which it is his or her duty to discover and develop. Our central aim as individuals is the refinement of our characters and the acquisition of those uniquely human qualities which we associate with our spiritual nature, or which have been traditionally referred to as 'saintly'. These divine qualities and attributes we must learn from our study of sacred scripture and from the example of the great religious teachers of all traditions. As our understanding of these qualities grows, we must try to uncover them in our own potential and to develop and apply them in our lives.

Significantly, these same spiritual qualities, such as love, forgiveness, justice and compassion are precisely those which help people to live together, to become unified. It is these qualities which make possible the higher levels of human interaction required to build an organic world society. Human beings are not inherently aggressive; aggressiveness is a distortion of the human spirit rooted in the anxiety and frustration of not being able to fulfil our human potential. Launch man on a constructive process of human development, and his aggressiveness will fade away. The individual spiritual development that is the basic aim of all religion is thus an essential component of our evolutionary progression towards a more ecologically balanced world.

We also have a social purpose, to carry forward an ever-advancing civilization. The social purpose of religion has often been forgotten as social and cultural conditions have changed, leading to an over-emphasis on individual salvation. Today the rapid development of material civilization makes the needs which would have to be met by this social purpose virtually self-evident. However civilization is not just material development, it also encompasses social structures and institutions. In that sense, civilization means working together, building communities, helping with the advancement of the whole human race. Today individual spiritual growth can best be achieved not by retiring to a cloistered life of contemplation, but by participating actively in society; not by celibacy, but by building true unity in the family. The threat of nuclear holocaust has made poignantly clear that salvation today is a group affair; either we save civilization together, or we all go together.

For anyone contemplating the environmental problems which threaten us, and the enormous human effort that will be required to resolve them, it is clear that the crucial question is one of motivation. Science can discover the solutions to all these problems, but where can we find the motivation necessary to implement the changes required? Building the necessary world society will require immense effort, solidarity, and sacrifice. The well-to-do may need to accept a reduction in their standard of living if resources are to be freed to raise the living standards of the poor and to bring down their population growth rate. Breaking down the barriers between peoples, nations, races, classes and religions requires courage and determination. It is not easy to leave the comfort and predictability of our own kind to associate with people whom we do not understand. What desire, what goal is strong enough to make us do these things?

All through history, religion has been one of the most powerful forces in the advancement of human civilization. The fact that its motivating power has often been perverted cannot disguise the powerful role that religion has played in the direction of society. It is not easy for us to judge this today, since religion, like any other institution, gradually loses its force, like a hearth in which the flame has died down, and the smouldering cinders lingering in the modern world produce more smoke than light. Even the bright sparks of individual pure souls are no longer sufficient to rekindle the flame of pure faith.

The essence of all revealed religions is a belief in something beyond ourselves, described by names which vary according to language and culture, such as God, Allah, or Jehovah. This is something associated with goodness, perfection, and absolute truth, but also something essentially unknown and unknowable, something which exceeds our ability to visualize and comprehend. This is reasonable, since we can only understand what we have experienced. Even our language, the very instrument of our thought processes and conceptualization, is only a reflection of human experience in the physical world. We try to extend it to abstract things by the use of symbol and metaphor, but these too have their limits. It is no wonder that attempts to codify spiritual truth have only led to division; spiritual experience is ultimately a very personal thing, difficult to communicate to others, and at least as variable as the rest of human experience.

This central concept – unknown and unknowable – is the key to human development, because religion teaches us to desire it, to love it, to worship it, to be full of positive feelings towards it. It is natural to be afraid of the unknown. Every child has been afraid of the dark, of a wolf in the corner or a monster under the bed, because what is dark is unseen and thus unknown. Fear of the unknown can paralyze us individually and socially. We all know people whose daily life is a simple routine, who are afraid to try anything new and unknown. Prejudices are based on fear of the unknown, of someone who is different from us in race, culture, class, religion or nationality. This is how the physical, animal, instinctual aspect of human nature reacts to the unknown.

In contrast, it is love *for* the unknown that gives religious belief its revolutionary potential and its capacity to transform human motivation and development. Individually, love for the unknown potential in ourselves motivates us to discover what that potential is. Instead of being afraid to try something new or different, we see it as an opportunity to learn something more about ourselves, to acquire new qualities and capacities. Failure is then accepted as just part of the learning process, of discovering what we can or cannot do, of probing our limits. Socially, the result is the same. Instead of being repelled by others who are different, we are drawn to them, overcoming our prejudices in the desire to discover more of the richness of human experience. In this context, education becomes particularly important, because it is the process of uncovering the unknown potential in ourselves and others. Scientific research too is exploring the unknown in the physical world, inventing new technologies and thereby advancing civilization.

Without this spiritual foundation of positive feelings for the unknown, we are handicapped in our development. Hemmed in by emotions which block our growth, we accumulate tensions which interfere with our social relationships. We cannot fulfil our individual or social potential.

Religion, as it is understood in the Bahá'í Faith, is thus, in essence, completely ecological. It leads to better adapted human beings. It lays the foundations for community relationships which can evolve towards higher levels of interconnectedness and efficiency. It inspires creativity and initiative, which produce the advances – the mutations – which are the basis of our social and cultural evolution.

It also traces out the moral values which must support the structures of a world social system, without which harmonious relationships are impossible. The first of these is justice, the foundation principle of social equilibrium. This means giving proper consideration to the claims of everyone concerned. If all human affairs are weighed in the light of justice, the principal sources of conflict and contention in the world will be removed. The many adjustments necessary to create a stable world society will only be possible if everyone sees that they are being treated equally and fairly. If sacrifices are necessary, they must be equitably distributed. Where an effort is needed, all must be seen to be doing their part.

Love for the whole human race, expressed as a sense of the oneness of mankind, is another essential value. We must come to feel as a single human social organism, as parts of the same body, each sharing some responsibility for the well-being of the whole. Just as in the human body it is not possible for a leg to be broken and an arm to say, 'That doesn't concern me, I'm fine', so it should be inconceivable that one human community could be suffering without all the others arising to help it. We must cultivate our sense of solidarity with the whole human family, just as we do with our own family. We must become conscious of the ecological relations which unite us, and work to strengthen them.

The primary human motivation must be one of service. We should not be thinking of ourselves and our personal advancement, but how we can best be of service to others. This implies an obligation to work, to make some constructive contribution to society. Idleness and living off others would be unacceptable, being unjust to those who work. This also involves courtesy and compassion, qualities which may seem old-fashioned, but which have proven their worth over the centuries in helping society function more smoothly.

Another obvious ecological value is moderation. Any good quality or discovery, if carried to excess, can become harmful. Moderation is the key to maintaining a balance with nature and within society. Renewable resources must be used in moderation. Pollution can often be released in moderation. Material development should be kept within the bounds of moderation. The same principle applies to the refinement of character, to arts and entertainment, to behaviour and government.

Religion, at least in the western world, is not commonly associated with a love for nature, yet the natural world is also a reflection of the qualities and attributes of that unknowable perfection which is its guiding force. Retirement into the wilderness has long been sought for meditation, contemplation and spiritual renewal. The richness, diversity and beauty of nature are there to be studied and admired. Love and compassion must be shown to every living creature. This too contributes to our growth and development.

Humanity and Nature

Bahá'u'lláh loved the beauty of the countryside. At one time during his imprisonment he remarked:

> I have not gazed on verdure for nine years. The country is the world of the soul, the city is the world of bodies.[25]

For Bahá'ís, while nature is not an end in itself to be worshipped and adored,[26] the creation does reflect the qualities and attributes of God.

> When . . . thou dost contemplate the innermost essence of all things, and the individuality of each, thou wilt behold the signs of thy Lord's mercy in every created thing, and see the spreading rays of His Names and Attributes throughout all the realm of being . . . Then wilt thou observe that the universe is a scroll that discloseth His hidden secrets, which are preserved in the well-guarded Tablet. And not an atom of all the atoms in existence, not a creature from amongst the creatures but speaketh His praise and telleth of His attributes and names, revealeth the glory of His might and guideth to His oneness and His mercy . . .
>
> And whensoever thou dost gaze upon creation all entire, and dost observe the very atoms thereof, thou wilt note that the rays of the Sun of Truth are shed upon all things and shining within them, and telling of that Day-Star's splendours, Its mysteries, and the spreading of Its lights. Look thou upon the trees, upon the blossoms and fruits, even upon the stones. Here too wilt thou behold the Sun's rays shed upon them, clearly visible within them, and manifested by them.[27]

The contemplation of nature thus has deep spiritual significance for Bahá'ís. Indeed interrelation of the spiritual, social and physical environments lies at the heart of the Bahá'í principle of oneness, which should be reflected in all human thought and activity.

> We cannot segregate the human heart from the environment outside us and say that once one of these is reformed everything will be improved. Man is organic with the world. His inner life moulds the environment and is itself also deeply affected by it. The one acts upon the other and every abiding change in the life of man is the result of these mutual reactions.[28]

The genetic diversity which underlies the richness of living things is a reflection of the qualities of God. 'Abdu'l-Bahá goes so far as to state that diversity is

> . . . the essence of perfection and the cause of the appearance of the bestowals of the Most Glorious Lord.[29]

We thus are encouraged to appreciate the diversity of the natural world, not only for its own sake, but also as a metaphor for the beauty and wonder inherent in the variety of human cultures.

> Consider the world of created beings, how varied and diverse they are in species, yet with one sole origin. All the differences that appear are those of outward form and colour. This diversity of type is apparent throughout the whole of nature. . . .
> Let us look . . . at the beauty in diversity, the beauty of harmony, and learn a lesson from the vegetable creation. If you beheld a garden in which all the plants were the same as to form, colour and perfume, it would not seem beautiful to you at all, but, rather, monotonous and dull. The garden which is pleasing to the eye and which makes the heart glad, is the garden in which are growing side by side flowers of every hue, form and perfume, and the joyous contrast of colour is what makes for charm and beauty. So is it with trees. An orchard full of fruit trees is a delight; so is a plantation planted with many species of shrubs. It is just the diversity and variety that constitutes its charm; each flower, each tree, each fruit, beside being beautiful in itself, brings out by contrast the qualities of the others, and shows to advantage the special loveliness of each and all.[30]

This appreciation of the importance, beauty and value of diversity is also, in the Bahá'í view, a vital consideration in the governance of human affairs. The very presence of differing personalities, classes, cultures and beliefs unlocks new potential in us all and demands the cultivation of new sensibilities and a heightened awareness of the impact we have on others and on the environment. We need others, so that we can come to a fuller understanding of who we are, and realize our true identity as part of the family of humanity.

Respect for the natural world is also reflected in the prohibition of cruelty to animals found in the Bahá'í writings:

> . . . it is not only their fellow human beings that the beloved of God must treat with mercy and compassion, rather must they show forth the utmost loving-kindness to every living creature. . . . The feelings are one and the same, whether ye inflict pain on man or on beast. . . . Train your children from their earliest days to be infinitely tender and loving to animals. If an animal be sick, let the children try to heal it, if it be hungry, let them feed it, if thirsty, let them quench its thirst, if weary, let them see that it rests.[31]

Similarly, we are counselled

> Unless ye must
> Bruise not the serpent in the dust
> How much less wound a man.
> And if ye can
> No ant should ye alarm
> Much less a brother harm.[32]

Such words remind us of the profound relationship between our attitudes towards other creatures and our attitudes towards our fellow human beings. We must recognize our interdependence with the natural world and that we cannot separate ourselves from it. Ultimately, we must overcome our egocentric view that places us above the natural world, and cultivate a sense of humility towards nature and all its treasures.

> Every man of discernment, while walking upon the earth, feeleth indeed abashed, inasmuch as he is fully aware that the thing which is the source of his prosperity, his wealth, his might, his exaltation, his advancement and power is, as ordained by God, the very earth which is trodden beneath the feet of all men. There can be no doubt that whoever is cognizant of this truth, is cleansed and sanctified from all pride, arrogance, and vainglory.[33]

The love for beauty, harmony and balance inspired by the

Bahá'í teachings extends to the creation of places of beauty, such as the Bahá'í World Centre, and Bahá'í Houses of Worship.

The historic and administrative sites at the Bahá'í World Centre in Israel's twin cities of Haifa and 'Akká have been embellished with gardens and buildings of spectacular beauty, and will continue to be developed and improved for many years to come. Long recognized as one of the Holy Land's most beautiful and peaceful scenes, the Bahá'í World Centre draws visitors from around the world. For Bahá'ís it is a place of pilgrimage, prayer and meditation, associated with the lives and sacrifices of the founding figures of their faith. Even those visitors who know little if anything of the historical associations of the Bahá'í World Centre are moved by the beauty and harmony of the formal gardens and buildings.

Bahá'í Houses of Worship are noted for their unique architecture and their adaptation to their environment. One of the best known of all Bahá'í temples is the most recently dedicated to public worship (December 1986), at New Delhi, India. Taking advantage of the freedom offered by new construction techniques, it shows the triumph of spirit and imagination over the mundane. Built in the form of a giant lotus flower, it has been hailed as one of the most astonishing feats of architecture and construction of the twentieth century. As the architect, Fariburz Sahba put it,

> In India, everyone respects the lotus flower. All religions accept it as a symbol of beauty, purity and the manifestation of God. So this temple really crystallized the concept of the Bahá'í Faith – that there is a great universality to all religions.[34]

Spiritual Nature

The ties between the natural world and our spiritual nature are very deep. The Bahá'í sacred writings abound with images and symbols drawn from nature, illustrating the intimate link between the material and spiritual worlds. By using the Bahá'í writings for prayer, meditation and study, we can develop a deeper understanding of spiritual truth through metaphors drawn from the natural world:

O God! We are as plants and Thy bounty is as the rain; refresh and cause these plants to grow through Thy bestowal.[35]

Bahá'u'lláh refers to his coming as the 'Divine Springtime',[36] and to himself as 'the Tree of Life that bringeth forth the fruits of God',[37] the 'Sun of Truth',[38] and 'the royal Falcon on the arm of the Almighty', who unfolds the drooping wings of every broken bird and starts it on its flight.[39] He represents his own revelation in symbolic terms as an ocean, with its attendant imagery of profundity, mystery, awe, power, and fertility:

My holy, My divinely ordained Revelation may be likened unto an ocean in whose depths are concealed innumerable pearls of great price, of surpassing lustre.[40]

Immerse yourselves in the ocean of My words, that ye may unravel its secrets, and discover all the pearls of wisdom that lie hid in its depths.[41]

This is the Ocean out of which all seas have proceeded, and with which every one of them will ultimately be united.[42]

Bahá'ís are urged to be as united as '. . . the rays of one sun, as the waves of one ocean, and as the fruit of one tree.'[43] Those passages devoted to personal ethics frequently use the image of cultivation:

In the garden of thy heart plant naught but the rose of love, and from the nightingale of affection and desire loosen not thy hold.[44]

Sow the seeds of My divine wisdom in the pure soil of thy heart, and water them with the water of certitude, that the hyacinths of My knowledge may spring up fresh and green in the sacred city of thy heart.[45]

Ye are the trees of My garden; ye must give forth goodly and wondrous fruits, that ye yourselves and others may profit therefrom.[46]

The fruits of the human tree are exquisite, highly desired and dearly cherished. Among them are upright character, virtuous deeds and a goodly utterance.[47]

'Abdu'l-Bahá states that

> Civilization has brought [man] out of his wild state just as
> the wild fruits which are cultivated by a gardener become
> finer, sweeter and acquire more freshness and delicacy.
> The gardeners of the world of humanity are the Prophets
> of God.[48]

In his writings, Bahá'u'lláh gave a voice to the earth itself,
contrasting its humility and generosity with our arrogance
and pride:

> 'I am to be preferred above you. For witness, how patient I
> am in bearing the burden which the husbandman layeth
> upon me. I am the instrument that continually imparteth
> unto all beings the blessings with which He Who is the
> Source of all grace hath entrusted me. Notwithstanding the
> honour conferred upon me, and the unnumbered evi-
> dences of my wealth – a wealth that supplieth the needs of
> all creation – behold the measure of my humility, witness
> with what absolute submissiveness I allow myself to be
> trodden beneath the feet of men.'[49]

Such natural symbols provide universal metaphors, which
have the capacity to unite all people.

The Bahá'í writings embody universally accessible ecological values which define the goals of our evolutionary
development, and give us the motivation necessary to
undertake the difficult and painful processes of individual
and social growth and the reorientation of civilization.
These values must be learned through education, the
process which gives us a consciousness of the directions we
should take. Such education can take many forms, from
formal schooling and independent study to prayer and
meditation. Learning ecological values should be a life-long
activity, as we never cease to develop, and are always ready
for a new and deeper understanding of values in the light of
accumulated experience. Our education should have as its
goal the attainment not just of knowledge, but of wisdom –
that is, the appropriate use of knowledge. If at any point we
stop learning, we risk sliding backwards as we outgrow our
previous understanding. The continued reliance on old
and outmoded ways of thinking about the world and our
place in it is largely responsible for our current environ-

mental problems.

One of the root causes of the environmental crisis is humankind's loss or ignorance of those spiritual principles and values which should sustain our relationship with the world around us. The traditional systems of respect, born of intimate contact with nature, have collapsed. Their place has been taken by materialistic philosophies which have given rise to the modern attitudes and economic and political systems that are driving our planet to ruin. Only a rediscovery of these eternal spiritual and ecological values can create the necessary ground swell for change and ultimately shift the momentum of our society in a new and more sustainable direction.

> There are spiritual principles, or what some call human values, by which solutions can be found for every social problem. Any well-intentioned group can in a general sense devise practical solutions to its problems, but good intentions and practical knowledge are usually not enough. The essential merit of spiritual principle is that it not only presents a perspective which harmonizes with that which is immanent in human nature, it also induces an attitude, a dynamic, a will, an aspiration, which facilitate the discovery and implementation of practical measures.[50]

Such principles and values are far from utopian or peripheral: they are essential and central to the healing and future progress of our world. They provide the motivation without which effective action is not possible. Bahá'ís, wherever and under whatever circumstances they live, are united in their commitment to such principles and values as the basis of their own transformation and that of their communities.

8. The Community as an Ecological Unit

The individual is the basic unit of biological organization. It is through genetic change in individuals that biological evolution takes place, just as human creativity is expressed at an individual level. However, most plants and animals can only live and function within communities. It is the community, or its functional expression in an ecosystem, that is the basic ecological unit. Humankind is a social species, and it is through our gathering into ever larger communities that we have made such an impact on the environment. But just as human communities are a major part of the environmental problems of today, so too must they be part of the solution. Communities that feel close to and are in balance with their environment, that are responsible for their resources and able to exercise some control over them, will tend to protect their environment in their own self interest.

Changing the values and actions of individuals tends by itself to be ineffective. People have much more impact if they work together. The kind of basic change needed to solve environmental problems will be much more effective if it is reflected at the community level where individual actions become mutually reinforcing.

To understand how communities work, what better model is there than those natural communities which have evolved and been perfected over thousands or millions of years? A lake, forest or savanna ecosystem shows the ways that many different plants and animals live together effectively and productively.

The coral reef ecosystem is a good example. These are rich biological communities that flourish in clear warm tropical ocean waters. The reef is in fact a geological structure built from the accumulated skeletons of generations of reef organisms. The corals are colonial animals that make limestone skeletons. In addition there are coralline algae, plants which also secrete limestone skeletons, and many other organisms that contribute to the building of the reef. Like human beings that build their own environment in cities, the coral reef system creates for itself a desirable place to live. It thus has more influence over its environment than many ecosystems.

Coral reefs are very ancient ecosystems. They have had tens of millions of years to evolve complex and efficient ways of functioning. They are particularly interesting because they live and flourish in an environment very poor in resources. The beautiful blue lagoon of tourism posters and travel films is so blue and transparent because there is nothing in the water. It is essentially a biological desert. Yet the reef survives like an oasis despite this lack of resources. Several characteristics of the system make this possible.

Energy for the reef system comes from sunlight, that renewable energy source which is all around us. The reef is particularly efficient at absorbing and using solar energy. The fantastic forms of coral organisms with knobs and branches everywhere create large amounts of surface to absorb the light. Then that surface is generally covered by many layers of organisms. Plants and animals are piled on top of each other on the reef, even boring inside the reef limestone. Thus much of the light reaching the reef is absorbed and used to make food energy for the system. This energy is then transferred efficiently within the system. Complex food webs made up of many organisms use and reuse the food energy; relatively little food is lost from the system. In contrast, our present civilization is grossly inefficient in its use of energy.

Since the coral reef usually has few sources of nutrients accessible to it, it must carefully trap and then recycle any nutrients which are available. The reef surface is covered by innumerable tiny arms and mouths, ready to catch any planktonic plants or animals that may happen by in the ocean water, to add to the nutrient stock of the system. Any dead matter containing nutrients is also recycled quickly within the system. There are many nitrogen-fixing organisms that add constantly to the reef's supply of nitrates, and these too are recycled within the system. We are only just beginning to appreciate the values of recycling as opposed to generating large amounts of waste which we cannot dispose of. As many non-renewable resources run out, recycling will be the only way to build up stocks within our system.

The secret to all this efficiency lies in the symbioses, the close working relationships between reef organisms. The corals are an excellent example. There are tiny plants, one-celled algae, living inside the coral animals. The corals build the structures that hold the plants out where there is plenty of light; they provide a comfortable, protected environment, and their waste products are recycled directly as fertilizer for the algae. In return, the algae provide a convenient supply of food products to the corals, who do not even have to eat in order to get them. What could be more efficient?

Another example is the relationship between the clown fish and the sea anemone. The sea anemone is an animal attached to the reef, with a mouth in the middle and a ring of tentacles with which it paralyses and eats fish. The clown fish is small but with brightly coloured orange, black, and white stripes that make it very visible, not necessarily a good idea when there are so many predatory fish on the reef. For some unknown reason, the clown fish is not paralyzed by the anemone, and it lives quite happily among the poisonous tentacles. The two work together. The clown fish swims back and forth above the anemone until a hungry fish comes along to eat it. At the last moment, it dives down into the anemone's tentacles; the hapless predator follows, is paralyzed and eaten by the anemone, and the clown fish shares in the table scraps. The anemone is fed in return for the protection and food it provides for the clown fish. The relationship can go much further. A researcher put a clownfish and an anemone in a tank without other fish. When the anemone became hungry, the clown fish searched the tank, found some food, and carried it back to feed its anemone. Thus solidarity and co-operation are very much part of the efficient coral reef ecosystem.

A coral reef is also one of the richest ecosystems in terms of the density of different kinds of species in a small area.

Hundreds of different kinds of coral, fish, other animals, and algae are crowded together on a typical reef. This is a true example of unity in diversity. Each organism has its different role in the reef system, and each contributes in some special way to the complex relationships which maintain the stability and productivity of the system. Even the different parts of the reef have specialized contributions to make to the whole, just as the different nations of the world will draw on their own situation and resources to make a unique contribution to a stable world system.

Coral reefs also play an important role in the maintenance of the global life support systems of the planet. The limestone skeletons which build the reef are formed from calcium carbonate, made by the reef organisms from the carbon dioxide available in sea water. Reefs are therefore an important sink or depository for carbon dioxide, particularly significant at a time when excess carbon dioxide from human activities is threatening major changes in the climate through the greenhouse effect.

Finally, the existence of ecosystems such as coral reefs demonstrates that continuing growth and development of a system are possible, despite lack of resources, by increasing the productivity, efficiency and integration of the system. There are thus probably no fixed limits to growth, but limits that can be modified and extended, allowing the development of ever greater and richer human societies if we follow a similar model. The example of the coral reef illustrates many basic features of an effective community structure. However, in drawing a parallel with human societies, a basic question rests. How do we humans form communities which can share such features?

It is in this area that the Bahá'í Faith has a particularly unique and creative solution to offer. While most religions today, particularly in the West, focus almost exclusively on individual spiritual development, the Bahá'í Faith recognizes the importance of community life and social organization. It lays out a whole new pattern for future society with an 'organic' structure that has much in common with natural systems such as the coral reef or the symbiotic relationship of the clown fish and sea anemone:

Because the members of the world of humanity are unable to exist without being banded together, co-operation and mutual helpfulness is the basis of human society. Without the realization of these two great principles no great movement is pressed forward.[51]

An effective community structure for environmental management must incorporate great decentralization, with local autonomy, responsibility and initiative to adapt to the particular requirements of each unique local environment. At the same time, each local community's activities must be harmonized with those of adjacent communities at a larger geographic scale, since many effects go well beyond the local area. Finally, there needs to be an effective structure to manage those resources and global systems which stabilize and renew the biosphere to maintain a healthy environment for all life. There is already in existence a remarkable model for such a structure, a model which has been 100 years in the making. The Bahá'í administrative order provides for such a decentralized but co-ordinated system at the local, national and international levels.

A Pattern of Administration

More important, perhaps, than the structure of a social system is the process by which it functions. An ecosystem is linked by flows of materials along food chains, by behavioural interactions, by mutual dependence and other relations in space and in time. Such ecological systems only function if interactions take place; it is the interactions which define the system. Since human evolution is now taking place primarily at a conscious intellectual and spiritual level, it is the intellectual and spiritual interchange between individuals through consultation that makes the social system function. Consultation is thus the social mechanism through which ecological values can be applied.

Most past methods for such an interchange have been restricted and imperfect, usually providing for the participation of a limited few who held power, or allowing communication only in one direction down a chain of command. The Bahá'í system of consultation, with regular community meetings at which everyone has the right to speak, plus consultative administrative bodies at all levels of human organization, provides for the most comprehensive possible pooling of the diverse viewpoints of mankind in a search for a more complete and balanced view of any situation. In Bahá'í consultation, the fullest possible expression of ideas is sought in an atmosphere of love and mutual respect, in a search for truth that is more encompassing than any one particular viewpoint. Such a process ensures the application of spiritual values to all aspects of society.

The Bahá'í writings not only suggest the principles to be applied in our social evolution towards a world system, they also lay out a pattern for administrative institutions that are freed from many of the deficiencies of present systems of government. Baha'i administration is carried out by consultative bodies, generally of nine members, at the local, national and international levels. The members of these bodies are elected by secret ballot, without any form of electioneering such as nominations or campaigning, from among all the members of the community: those who are elected have an obligation to serve. The community thus chooses those of its members in whom they have the greatest confidence, and those elected are responsible only to their own conscience and to God, not to an electorate. All decisions are made collectively after prayerful consultation and a free exchange of views, and are motivated by the search for truth and the application of spiritual principles. There is no place in this system for individuals who seek special power, rank or authority. Authority lies with the institution, not with the individuals who comprise it. Election to a Bahá'í administrative institution is based on principles of service and humility, requiring such qualities as detachment, selflessness, maturity, and sincerity, and cannot be looked upon as acknowledgement of inherent superiority or a means of self-advancement.

Such a system is best able to draw on the full diversity of talents within the community, from the grass roots to the highest levels of international organization. It balances global co-ordination with the greatest possible decentralization and local autonomy, allowing each component to reflect its own particular attributes and characteristics. This type of system is becoming an ideal agent for change. It provides a means whereby individual needs can be linked to wider social goals. It puts people in charge of their own destiny, and gets them involved in the process of transformation. It both makes the application of ecological principles possible, and reflects them in its own structure and workings.

The Bahá'í teachings even lay down principles for the physical organization of communities which make them more organic in structure and function. A House of Worship provides a spiritual centre for community life, where people can gather together in prayer and meditation before going to their daily occupations. In future these Houses of Worship will be surrounded by the social institutions of community life: school, library, hospital, general storehouse, etc. The locally elected governing body, known as the Spiritual Assembly, will provide for the needs of all members of the community, receiving revenues graduated on the basis of ability to pay, and distributing necessities to those unable to provide for themselves. Such communities are providing the foundation for a new world social system, responsive both to the human needs of the people and the requirements of the environment.

9. An Organically United World

The leaders and peoples of the world have finally taken stock of the mounting scientific evidence and realized that the whole planet is threatened by environmental imbalances caused by human activities. For the first time human beings are in danger, not from local or regional problems from which we can escape, but from our own world-wide impact. It is becoming increasingly clear that such global problems require global solutions. However, the form that such solutions should take and the means for applying them are still unclear.

Building a world society will require functional changes in human systems, changes which will mean further evolutionary steps in the scale, the integration and the efficiency of human communities. Creating new levels of integration in human affairs will involve painstaking efforts. In particular, means must be found to give form to the need for global management of the environment. The kinds of changes required in governmental structures, economic and technological systems, and social relations are so radical as to amount to a revolution in human society. Yet as with biological revolutions, such as the development of warm-bloodedness in the first mammals, the new potential opened up by these changes will be enormous.

Structural Changes

Nothing in this world of existence is exempt from the law of change. Human institutions, like organisms, are founded to meet a particular set of environmental conditions. As the environment changes, those institutions must either adapt or perish. The institution of unlimited national sovereignty and the structures that uphold it were meant to serve humanity; we should not sacrifice humanity today to uphold a supposedly inviolable institution.

World unity requires organic changes at all levels of human society, changes that have been foreshadowed in the Bahá'í writings. A world federal system will be required, with the political, executive and judicial institutions necessary to regulate the relations between nations, to prevent war, and to manage the resources of the entire planet for the good of all. Such a system will be able to tap and fully utilize the sources of raw materials and regulate the distribution of products. It will be able to exploit the unused and unsuspected resources and all available sources of energy on the surface of the planet, for ultimately energy will become the most limiting resource for the world system. Only such a structure will be able to manage the biosphere and its component global systems.

A world economic system will also have to be developed, with a single currency and complete freedom of trade between countries. Such a system will allow maximum efficiency in the production and distribution of goods and services, adapted to the resources and capacities of each region of the world. This will eliminate the enormous cost of the inefficiencies of the present system, which maintains much uneconomic production for self-interest and for supposed reasons of national security. It will also allow the application of the principle of justice in the distribution of resources, eliminating the extremes of wealth and poverty that divide nations today. Only then will each nation be able to find its true place in the world system.

The result is an organic pattern for world society, much like biological systems. The world level of organization corresponds to those life support systems which maintain the whole planet in a healthy state for life. The nations are equivalent to the great biogeographic provinces which share common climatic and biological elements in one geographic region. The cities and rural communities are like ecosystems, organized to meet most of their needs from within the system. The many human trades and specializations that together contribute to a functioning community can be compared to the species. The individuals are the units of productivity, creativity and initiative in both systems, since it is primarily at this level that evolution first operates.

Such an organic structure is inherently decentralized, with a high degree of local differentiation and adaptation. The efficiency of such a structure has been proved over millions of years of biological evolution. There is no reason why such a pattern should not serve equally well for world society.

The Baha'i view contains not only a vision of this kind of society, but also a realistic assessment of the measures that must be applied and the steps that must be followed to achieve the ultimate goal of a new world civilization. That view is much broader than those usually considered by environmental scientists, yet it is consistent with a scientific view of the problem. Indeed, it can find inspiration in what natural systems have themselves accomplished. The Bahá'í view is also positive. At a time when current trends offer strong grounds for pessimism and despair, a longer perspective that gives hope for the future is both an antidote for those negative feelings and a motivation to work for the changes needed.

The significance of the Bahá'í view is that it is rooted in a profound understanding of the evolutionary processes at work in human society. It places today's environmental problems in their proper perspective. It is clear from this perspective that the solutions to these problems lie not in specifically environmental activities, important as these may be, but in a complete restructuring of human society. Until the necessary steps are taken in this direction, little can be done to solve the global environmental crisis. In the words of Bahá'u'lláh,

> The well-being of mankind, its peace and security, are unattainable unless and until its unity is firmly established. This unity can never be achieved so long as the counsels which the Pen of the Most High hath revealed are suffered to pass unheeded.[52]

Solutions to the environment crisis, and the other grave problems threatening mankind, will only prove possible once the nations have united in a world federal system, not before.

Environmental Justice

A new foundation of global moral values must support the structural changes necessary for a united world. The moral dimension of environmental problems has too frequently been divorced from the scientific, yet the two are complementary and mutually reinforcing. The science of the environment is demonstrating new human responsibilities and obligations in areas that previously were taken for granted because they were beyond the scope of human action. There was no need for a human right to have air fit to breathe when air seemed unlimited and free. Today in some cities, that right is seriously constrained.

The fundamental moral principles of justice and 'the golden rule', 'do unto others as you would have others do unto you', are universal, but their applications must evolve with the changing times. In the Bahá'í view, we must come to see all humanity as part of an interrelated whole. Just as a human body is made up of many cells, tissues, organs and structures, so the human race is composed of many races, peoples and nations, yet all today form part of the same global system. If one part of a body suffers, the whole organism suffers. Humanity has become like that body. It is no longer possible to ignore the suffering of people anywhere in the world. That same sense of interrelatedness must apply to the world environment, which is itself becoming one of the causes of much human suffering. New concepts of environmental justice must be developed and become reflected in legislation and administration.

For instance, environmental abuse tends to give benefits to one group while imposing costs on others. The owner of a factory may make more money if he does not install pollution control equipment; the damage from the pollution will most likely affect others, not himself. Most societies accept the principle of liability for damages caused in other domains. The same must apply to environmental harm, through what is sometimes referred to as the 'polluter pays principle'. The issue is more complex when the harm is done by the cumulative effect of many sources of pollution, and individual liability is more difficult to demonstrate. Responsibility in such cases falls on the whole society.

Often it is the poor and defenseless who suffer most. They cannot afford to move away from the most polluted areas, nor do they have the means to fight for their rights. Environmental damage then becomes another form of unjust oppression and exploitation of the poor.

As impacts have spread, the environment has also become a significant dimension of international relations. Increasingly today pollution and other environmental impacts cross national boundaries, damaging resources and affecting human health in countries that have no control over the source of their problem. The aggrieved countries have no recourse other than the usual diplomatic protests. There is presently no international machinery for environmental liability and compensation apart from a few specialized conventions such as those covering pollution of the sea by ships. The most extreme situation is that of the small coral atoll states. The greenhouse effect, produced in large part by the high fossil fuel consumption in the developed countries, is expected to raise the sea-level sufficiently to cause these states to disappear, making their populations environmental refugees. At present they have no recourse against the damage they are going to suffer.

Environmental justice requires that such situations be resolved, but no wealthy person, company or country wants to support legislation that will require it to make heavy payments in compensation. Only when the wealthy and powerful realize that they too cannot escape the harmful consequences of their acts and that the survival of all is at stake will real efforts begin to be mobilized. That point seems to be coming. The number of international conferences on the environment is increasing, and some of the rhetoric about protecting the environment is being turned into action.

It is now increasingly recognized that among the fundamental human rights should be the right to a clean, healthy and productive environment. Such a right should be protected by law both nationally and internationally, and every effort made to restore it to the many millions who today suffer the indignities of a degraded and polluted world.

The morality of environmental conservation also applies to our responsibility to future generations. The selfish idea that all of the world is free for us to exploit here and now, without regard for the consequences, must give way to a broader sense of responsibility and stewardship. The idea that ownership is total and includes the right to destroy one's possessions must have its limits. If a wealthy eccentric bought up the world's greatest works of art and then set fire to them, we would be horrified. Somehow great art is seen as part of our global heritage, to be appreciated and passed on to our children and grandchildren. The same principle should apply to the world's productive capacity. The benefits we receive from our resources should not be at the expense of their future potential. Our present headlong rush to strip the planet of its wealth will certainly be regretted and condemned by our descendants.

The Bahá'í Community in Action

For nearly a century and a half, Bahá'ís have been building a new pattern for society based on principles outlined by Bahá'u'lláh. These efforts have now reached the point where several million people, representing most of the planet's races, nations, classes, cultures and languages, have created a pilot-scale, fully-functioning model, the embryo of a world community where these principles are seen in action. This has been accompanied by a growing awareness amongst Bahá'ís of the needs of the environment, and increasing involvement in its protection. First efforts were individually inspired, such as those of Richard St Barbe Baker, who founded the society 'Men of the Trees', which now has chapters throughout the world. Community action followed, such as the participation of the Bahá'í International Community in the United Nations Conference on the Human Environment and the related NGO Environment Forum in Stockholm in 1972, where it contributed a statement on 'The Environment and Human Values'. There is now permanent Bahá'í representation in Nairobi, the headquarters of the United Nations Environment Programme, and a newly-established Bahá'í Office of the Environment at the United Nations in New York.

At national and local levels, Bahá'í involvement in economic and social development has included many environmental activities, which are now assuming greater importance in their own right. Bahá'ís actively supported

European Environment Year (1987-8) with public meetings and with practical projects such as planting trees in fire-damaged forests, clearing trails, and cleaning up rivers. Educational audio-visual presentations aimed at increasing public awareness not only of the problems but also of viable solutions have been produced and used by Bahá'ís in several countries. World wide, many Bahá'í communities have undertaken agricultural, forestry and environmental health initiatives, such as the establishment of an environmental studies centre in Bolivia and the creation of an agroforestry project in India. Tree planting campaigns have been organized or supported by Bahá'ís in many countries including Benin, Canada, Chad, Ecuador, Haiti, India, Kenya, Laos and Madagascar. The environment is also the subject of a growing number of Bahá'í publications.

In recent years Bahá'ís have increasingly joined with other groups in developing public awareness of and involvement in environmental issues. Special conferences have been organized to bring together people from different movements and academic disciplines to establish common ground for united action. One of the most successful of these took place in September 1989, at the Bahá'í offices at the United Nations in New York, on 'Africa: Environment and Development', jointly sponsored by the Club of Rome, the United Nations Non-Governmental Liaison Service, and the Bahá'í International Community.

Bahá'ís all over the world are also promoting dialogue between religious communities for action on the environment. In 1987 the Bahá'í Faith was the sixth major religion to join the Network on Religion and Conservation, organized by the World Wide Fund for Nature (WWF), and on that occasion issued a *Bahá'í Declaration on Nature*. Bahá'ís also participate in the WWF pilgrimages to Canterbury Cathedral, at which the religious communities living in the United Kingdom avow their commitment to the preservation of the planet.

In October 1988 the Bahá'í International Community, in association with WWF UK, launched the 'Arts for Nature' campaign, to heighten awareness of the environmental crisis through the creative arts, and to enlist the talents of the artistic community in furthering conservation work.

The Universal House of Justice, in April 1989, called on all Bahá'ís to seek to conserve the environment in ways which blend with the rhythm of Bahá'í community life. There can be no doubt, therefore, that environmental issues will assume increasing importance for Bahá'ís all over the world, and that this will be reflected in their activities in the years ahead.

The Future

As scientists and political leaders search for the solutions to major threats to our environment, they may find in the Bahá'í example a source of inspiration for their work, and a model for a sustainable global society. As the Bahá'í community continues to grow and expand, and as these principles are applied to the problems of the present world, so enormous new potential is released for the building of an ever-advancing and environmentally harmonious world civilization.

The experience of the Bahá'í community offers real hope to those who despair at finding solutions to the world's environmental problems. Bahá'ís are people from all races, cultures, religious backgrounds and walks of life who see the world as one country. They share a common system of ethics and values which embraces the varied elements of human society, and develops, as no other faith or ideology has done, a living sense of responsibility for the planet. At the grass roots level Bahá'ís are striving to transform those materialistic philosophies and values whose expressions in present economic and political systems are ruining the global environment, and to provide the basis for a new, environmentally benign civilization. They are building organically functioning and evolving communities, able to take on responsibility for local environmental conservation. By cultivating more creative responses to the new challenges offered by the world around us, Bahá'ís have embarked on a process of educating themselves and their children to live as planetary citizens.

To become a Bahá'í means, in part, to accept responsibility for one's own development, and it is the goal of every Bahá'í community to foster and release the potential of each of its members. Those people who are generally brushed aside by the dominant social structures of East and

West, such as women, the elderly, the underprivileged, children, the disabled, and ethnic minorities, are particularly valued and nurtured in Bahá'í communities. This gives Bahá'í communities a richness and diversity that is part of their strength, allowing them to draw on all the available resources in the community.

Every person is capable of making their own distinctive contribution towards society by developing their innate talents and capacities: the Bahá'í way of life empowers people to do this. Such a task requires patience, hope, confidence, and the courage to challenge old, outworn and harmful attitudes. The most harmful attitude of all, which has long dominated our understanding of our own nature, is that we are inherently aggressive and war-like.

> There is . . . a paralysis of will; and it is this that must be carefully examined and resolutely dealt with. This paralysis is rooted . . . in a deep-seated conviction of the inevitable quarrelsomeness of mankind, which has led to the reluctance to entertain the possibility of subordinating national self-interest to the requirements of world order, and in an unwillingness to face courageously the far-reaching implications of establishing a united world authority.[53]

Bahá'ís have resolved this 'paralysis of will' in themselves. They have rejected the cynicism and pessimism inherent in the traditional view of human nature, and challenge the rest of the world to do the same.

With its emphasis on unity, co-operation and consensus, the Bahá'í community offers a dynamic pattern for future society. Bahá'ís believe, on the evidence of more than a century of their own experience, that a common resolve can be forged, and that words can be translated into actions. The effort required to avert the environmental crisis is more significant than just a response to a temporary, though serious emergency. It may in fact push nations into precedent-setting measures for the creation of effective international institutions and legislation. It will be a painful process, but it will elevate society to a new level of global integration and cooperation, and will help reveal the true identity, nobility and beauty of the human race.

Humanity is moving out of its collective adolescence towards maturity: we are slowly but surely coming of age, and are all beginning to realize our true identity as one people with one common home.

The threats to the ecological balance of the planet are symptoms of the materialism, disunity and inequality in the modern world. The reconstruction of human society will require both the rediscovery and development of our spiritual nature and the union of all the nations in the best interests of all humankind. If we are to move beyond our immediate environmental crisis we must accept the oneness of humanity and our oneness with the natural world, a world where, in the words of Bahá'u'lláh, we are all 'the fruits of one tree, and the leaves of one branch.'[54]

References

Chapter 1
1. 'Abdu'l-Bahá, *Some Answered Questions*. Wilmette, Bahá'í Publishing Trust, 5th edition, 1981, page 180.
2. Bahá'u'lláh, 'Tablet of Wisdom', published in *Tablets of Bahá'u'lláh Revealed After the Kitáb-i-Aqdas*. Bahá'í World Centre, revised edition, 1982, page 140.
3. 'Abdu'l-Bahá, *Some Answered Questions*, pages 180-1.
4. Ibid., pages 181-2.
5. Ibid., page 182-3.
6. Bahá'u'lláh, *Tablets of Bahá'u'lláh*, page 142.
7. 'Abdu'l-Bahá, *Some Answered Questions*, page 3.
8. 'Abdu'l-Bahá, *Bahá'í World Faith*. Wilmette, Bahá'í Publishing Trust, 1956, page 242.
9. 'Abdu'l-Bahá, *Some Answered Questions*, pages 198-9.
10. Ibid., pages 193-4.
11. Ibid., page 199.
12. Ibid., pages 178-9.
13. 'Abdu'l-Bahá, quoted in 'Extracts on Protection of the Environment and the Relationship of Man with Nature.' (unpublished compilation from the Bahá'í World Centre).

Chapter 2
14. 'Abdu'l-Bahá, quoted in *Conservation of the Earth's Resources*. London, Bahá'í Publishing Trust, 1990, page 4.
15. Bahá'u'lláh, *Epistle to the Son of the Wolf*. Wilmette, Bahá'í Publishing Trust, revised edition, 1979, page 55.

Chapter 3
16. 'Abdu'l-Bahá, *Selections from the Writings of 'Abdu'l-Bahá*. Haifa, Bahá'í World Centre, revised edition, 1982, page 302.
17. See The Universal House of Justice, *The Promise of World Peace*. London, Bahá'í Publishing Trust, 1985, pages 2-3.

Chapter 5
18. 'Abdu'l-Bahá, *Foundations of World Unity*. Wilmette, Bahá'í Publishing Trust, 1945, page 39.
19. 'Abdu'l-Bahá, quoted in *Star of the West*, National Spiritual Assembly of the Bahá'ís of the USA, Volume 4, No 6, (24 June 1913), page 103 (George Ronald Publishers, bound volume, 1978)
20. 'Abdu'l-Bahá, quoted in *Conservation*, page 12.
21. 'Abdu'l-Bahá, quoted ibid.
22. 'Abdu'l-Bahá, quoted ibid.
23. Bahá'u'lláh, 'Tablet of the World', published in *Tablets*, pages 89-90.

Chapter 7
24. Bahá'u'lláh, *Gleanings from the Writings of Baha'u'lláh*, London, Bahá'í Publishing Trust, revised edition, 1978, pages 341-2.
25. Bahá'u'lláh, quoted in Esslemont, *Bahá'u'lláh and the New Era*. London: Bahá'í Publishing Trust, 1974, page 33.
26. See 'Abdu'l-Bahá, *Paris Talks; Addresses Given by 'Abdu'l-Bahá in Paris, 1911-12*, London, Bahá'í Publishing Trust, 1971 page 123.
27. 'Abdu'l-Bahá, *Selections*, pages 41-2.
28. Letter written on behalf of Shoghi Effendi, 17 February 1933, quoted in *Conservation*, page 15.
29. 'Abdu'l-Bahá, *Selections*, page 291.
30. 'Abdu'l-Bahá, *Paris Talks*, pages 51-3.
31. 'Abdu'l-Bahá, *Selections*, pages 158-9.
32. Ibid., page 256.
33. Bahá'u'lláh, *Epistle*, page 44.
34. Fariburz Sahba, quoted in *One Country; Newsletter of the Bahá'í International Community*. New York, Spring 1989, Vol 1, No 2, page 9.

35. 'Abdu'l-Bahá, *Bahá'í Prayers*. London, Bahá'í Publishing Trust, revised edition, 1975, page 93.
36. Bahá'u'lláh, *Gleanings*, page 27.
37. Bahá'u'lláh, 'Tablet of Aḥmad', published in *Bahá'í Prayers for Special Occasions*. London, Bahá'í Publishing Trust, revised fourth edition, 1975, page 47.
38. Bahá'u'lláh, *The Seven Valleys*. Wilmette, Bahá'í Publishing Trust, third revised edition, 1978, page 38.
39. Bahá'u'lláh, 'Tablet of Maqṣúd', published in *Tablets*, page 169.
40. Bahá'u'lláh, *Gleanings*, page 325.
41. Bahá'u'lláh, *Synopsis and Codification of the Laws and Ordinances of the Kitáb-i-Aqdas*. Haifa, Bahá'í World Centre, 1973, page 27.
42. Bahá'u'lláh, *Gleanings*, page 103.
43. 'Abdu'l-Bahá, *Bahá'í Prayers*, page 91.
44. Bahá'u'lláh, *The Hidden Words*. London, Bahá'í Publishing Trust, 1932, from the Persian, No 3.
45. Ibid., No 33.
46. Ibid., No 80.
47. Bahá'u'lláh, *Tablets*, page 257.
48. 'Abdu'l-Bahá, *Some Answered Questions*, page 194.
49. Bahá'u'lláh, *Gleanings*, page 8.
50. The Universal House of Justice, *The Promise of World Peace*, pages 15-16.

Chapter 8
51. 'Abdu'l-Bahá, quoted in *Bahá'í News*, National Spiritual Assembly of the Bahá'ís of the USA, July 1929, pages 1-2.

Chapter 9
52. Bahá'u'lláh, *Gleanings*, page 285.
53. The Universal House of Justice, *The Promise of World Peace*, page 11.
54. Bahá'u'lláh, *Gleanings*, page 217.

Appendix: A Bahá'í Declaration on Nature

Introduction

In September of 1986 the World Wide Fund for Nature (WWF) launched their Network on Conservation and Religion, bringing religious leaders representing Buddhists, Christians, Hindus, Jews and Muslims together with environmental leaders in Assisi, Italy.

Each of the five religions represented there issued a declaration on nature. As of October 1987, the Bahá'ís became the sixth major religion to join this new alliance, and put forward this statement in support of the Network's objectives:

> Nature in its essence is the embodiment of My Name, the Maker, the Creator. Its manifestations are diversified by varying causes, and in this diversity there are signs for men of discernment. Nature is God's Will and is its expression in and through the contingent world. It is a dispensation of Providence ordained by the Ordainer, the All-Wise.
>
> *Bahá'í Writings*

With these words, Bahá'u'lláh, Prophet-Founder of the Bahá'í Faith, outlines the essential relationship between man and the environment: that the grandeur and diversity of the natural world are purposeful reflections of the majesty and bounty of God. For Bahá'ís, there follows an implicit understanding that nature is to be respected and protected, as a divine trust for which we are answerable.

Such a theme, of course, is not unique to the Bahá'í Faith. All the world's major religions make this fundamental connection between the Creator and His creation. How could it be otherwise? All the major independent religions are based on revelations from one God – a God who has

93

successively sent His Messengers to earth so that humankind might become educated about His ways and will. Such is the essence of Bahá'í belief.

As the most recent of God's revelations, however, the Bahá'í teachings have a special relevance to present-day circumstances when the whole of nature is threatened by man-made perils ranging from the wholesale destruction of the world's rainforests to the final nightmare of nuclear annihilation.

A century ago, Bahá'u'lláh proclaimed that humanity has entered a new age. Promised by all the religious Messengers of the past, this new epoch will ultimately bring peace and enlightenment for humanity. To reach that point, however, humankind must first recognize its fundamental unity - as well as the unity of God and of religion. Until there is a general recognition of this wholeness and interdependence, humanity's problems will only worsen.

'The well-being of mankind, its peace and security, are unattainable unless and until its unity is firmly established', Bahá'u'lláh wrote. 'The earth is but one country, and mankind its citizens.'

The major issues facing the environmental movement today hinge on this point. The problems of ocean pollution, the extinction of species, acid rain and deforestation – not to mention the ultimate scourge of nuclear war – respect no boundaries. All require a transnational approach.

While all religious traditions point to the kind of cooperation and harmony that will indeed be necessary to curb these threats, the religious writings of the Bahá'í Faith also contain an explicit prescription for the kind of new world political order that offers the only long-term solution to such problems.

'That which the Lord hath ordained as the sovereign remedy and mightiest instrument for the healing of the world is the union of all its people in one universal cause.' Bahá'u'lláh wrote.

Built around the idea of a world commonwealth of nations, with an international parliament and executive to carry out its will, such a new political order must also, according to the Baha'i teachings, be based on principles of economic justice, equality between the races, equal rights for women and men, and universal education.

All these points bear squarely on any attempt to protect the world's environment. The issue of economic justice is an example. In many regions of the world, the assault on rainforests and endangered species comes as the poor, legitimately seeking a fair share of the world's wealth, fell trees to create fields. They are unaware that, over the long term and as members of a world community which they know little about, they may be irretrievably damaging rather than improving their children's chances for a better life. Any attempt to protect nature, must, therefore, also address the fundamental inequities between the world's rich and poor.

Likewise, the uplifting of women to full equality with men can help the environmental cause by bringing a new spirit of feminine values into decision-making about natural resources. The scriptures of the Bahá'í Faith note that:

> . . . man has dominated over woman by reason of his more forceful and aggressive qualities both of body and mind. But the balance is already shifting; force is losing its dominance, and mental alertness, intuition and the spiritual qualities of love and service, in which woman is strong, are gaining ascendancy. Hence the new age will be an age less masculine and more permeated with feminine ideals.

Education, especially an education that emphasizes Bahá'í principles of human interdependence, is another prerequisite to the building of a global conservation consciousness. The Faith's theology of unity and interdependence relates specifically to environmental issues. Again, to quote Bahá'í sacred writings:

> By nature is meant those inherent properties and necessary relations derived from the realities of things. And these realities of things, though in the utmost diversity, are yet intimately connected one with the other . . . Liken the world of existence to the temple of man. All the organs of the human body assist one another, therefore life continues . . . Likewise among the parts of existence there is a wonderful connection and interchange of forces which is the cause of life in the world and the continuation of the countless phenomena.

The very fact that such principles should come with the

authority of religion and not merely from human sources, is yet another piece of the overall solution to our environmental troubles. The impulse behind the Assisi declarations on nature is testimony to this idea.

There is perhaps no more powerful impetus for social change than religion. Bahá'u'lláh said: 'Religion is the greatest of all means for the establishment of order in the world and for the peaceful contentment of all that dwell therein.' In attempting to build a new ecological ethic, the teachings of all religious traditions can play a role in helping to inspire their followers.

Bahá'u'lláh, for example, clearly addresses the need to protect animals. 'Look not upon the creatures of God except with the eye of kindliness and of mercy, for Our loving providence hath pervaded all created things, and Our grace encompassed the earth and the heavens.'

He Himself expressed a keen love and appreciation for nature, furthering the connection between the environment and the spiritual world in Bahá'í theology. 'The country is the world of the soul, the city is the world of bodies', Bahá'u'lláh said.

This dichotomy between spirituality and materialism is a key to understanding the plight of humankind today. In the Bahá'í view, the major threats to our world environment, such as the threat of nuclear annihilation, are manifestations of a world-encompassing sickness of the human spirit, a sickness that is marked by an overemphasis on material things and a self-centredness that inhibits our ability to work together as a global community. The Bahá'í Faith seeks above all else to revitalize the human spirit and break down the barriers that limit fruitful and harmonious cooperation among men and women, whatever their national, racial or religious background.

For Bahá'ís the goal of existence is to carry forward an ever-advancing civilization. Such a civilization can only be built on an earth that can sustain itself. The Bahá'í commitment to the environment is fundamental to our Faith.